SAFFRON SHORES ★

SAFFRON SHORES

JEWISH COOKING OF THE SOUTHERN MEDITERRANEAN

by JOYCE GOLDSTEIN

photographs by LEIGH BEISCH

CHRONICLE BOOKS

SAN FRANCISCO

SAFFRON SHORES IS DEDICATED TO BARBARA TROPP.
SUPERB COOK, INSPIRED TEACHER, AND BELOVED FRIEND.

: :

TEXT COPYRIGHT © 2002 BY JOYCE GOLDSTEIN.

PHOTOGRAPHS COPYRIGHT © 2002 BY LEIGH BEISCH.

LIBRARY OF CONGRESS CATALOGING-IN-PUBLICATION
DATA AVAILABLE.

ISBN 0-8118-3052-7

MANUFACTURED IN CHINA

PROP STYLING BY SARA SLAVIN
FOOD STYLING BY SANDRA COOK
DESIGNED BY SARA SCHNEIDER
TYPESETTING BY KRISTEN WURZ
THE PHOTOGRAPHER WOULD LIKE TO THANK SUE FISHER KING, SUR LA
TABLE, AFIKOMEN JEWISH BOOKS AND GIFTS, AND MAISON MARRAKESH
FOR THEIR GENEROUS CONTRIBUTION OF PROPS.
WE CREATED THIS BOOK IN THE SHADOW OF THE SEPTEMBER 11TH
DISASTER. OUR HEARTS GO OUT TO ALL WHO HAVE BEEN AFFECTED, WE
WISH YOU STRENGTH AND PEACE.

DISTRIBUTED IN CANADA BY RAINCOAST BOOKS
9050 SHAUGHNESSY STREET
VANCOUVER, BC V6P 6E5

10 9 8 7 6 5 4 3 2 1

CHRONICLE BOOKS LLC
85 SECOND STREET
SAN FRANCISCO, CALIFORNIA 94105
WWW.CHRONICLEBOOKS.COM

contents

:::::: **INTRODUCTION**

Most Jews in America are of Ashkenazic origins; that is, their families come from Eastern and Central Europe. It is Ashkenazic cuisine that most Americans think of as Jewish food. Rib-sticking dishes such as matzoh ball soup, gefilte fish, brisket and latkes, kugel, challah, and rugelach are well known and well loved. Over the past twenty years, interest in Mediterranean food has been growing. Flavorful and healthful, it has been embraced by chefs and food companies alike. Because of this spotlight on the Mediterranean, the cuisine of the Sephardic, or Mediterranean, Jews is now getting the attention it deserves. *Sefarad* was the Hebrew name given to the Iberian peninsula in ancient times. Any Jewish food that is not Ashkenazic comes under this broad title. The term *Sephardic,* however, can apply to quite diverse cuisines and cultural influences. While the Ashkenazim maintained a rather closed community, the Sephardim were outgoing and participated actively in whatever community they lived in. They shared recipes and culinary traditions with their non-Jewish neighbors. Their food reflected the cuisine of their homeland but adapted to follow the kosher laws.

In my book *Cucina Ebraica: Flavors of the Italian Jewish Kitchen,* I wrote about the history of the Jews in Italy, where the Sephardim joined the *Italkim* (native Italian Jews) and *Ashkenazim* (Germanic Jews) and the Levantine Jews in such centers as Rome, Ferrara, and Venice. This Italian food showed the diverse influences of Sephardic and Ashkenazic roots, with the Sephardic dominating. In *Sephardic Flavors: Jewish Cooking of the Mediterranean,* I explored classic Sephardic (Judeo-Spanish) cuisine, which combines Turkish and Balkan cooking with that of Iberian Jews who settled in the Ottoman Empire, more of the Northern Mediterranean diaspora. My curiosity and palate piqued, I had to continue this culinary adventure and explore the food of the Jews who lived on the southern shores of the Mediterranean. I wanted to learn more about the Maghrebi cooking of the North African Jews, which incorporates the foods of Morocco, Algeria, Tunisia, and Libya. While not purely Sephardic, as much of this cuisine existed before the arrival of the Jews from the Iberian peninsula, the taste interplay between North Africa and the Iberian peninsula is evident in many a bite. Judeo-Arabic cooking, also considered Sephardic, has its roots in Syria, Lebanon, Iraq, and Iran. Sephardic cuisines defy narrow definition and description. Many of the dishes are distinctly regional, idiosyncratic from country to country, city to city. (Diversity is the key.) This book is about the sensual cuisines of Sephardic Jews in the Muslim lands of North Africa and the Arabic countries that line the saffron shores.

JEWS IN MUSLIM LANDS

History repeats itself. When the repeat patterns are favorable, we rejoice in the good fortune and wisdom of having learned from the past. When the patterns are unfortunate, we regret that progress has not been made and fear that we must live through a bad time yet again. The history of the Jews contains a bit of both. The theme song could be "Good Times, Bad Times." These alternating patterns have been repeated and repeated for thousands of years. As I worked on *Saffron Shores* and read of the complicated history of Jews in Muslim lands, I saw that progress has been made but that the pattern of conflict is ongoing and Jewish-Muslim relations are still unresolved and unsettled. What an old, old story this is.

Until the first century, most of the world's Jews lived in or near Jerusalem. Their spiritual, cultural, social, and economic life revolved around the Temple. Jews suffered greatly under Roman rule. In 70 C.E., the Romans laid siege to Jerusalem and destroyed the Temple. Many Jews were killed; those who remained became slaves or went into exile. The Jews in Jerusalem regrouped, codified the Hebrew Bible and oral tradition of study, and established the synagogue system. In 313 C.E. the Roman Emperor Constantine converted to Christianity and set about to make it the official religion of the Roman Empire. Not a good time for the Jews. In the seventh century, a new monotheistic religion developed. Muhammad spread his teachings far and wide in the Arab lands. Islam became the religion of the Middle East and North Africa. Jews remained a minority. During this time, most of the world's Jews lived in Babylonia, Persia, and the Middle East. Compared to their existence under Christianity, life for the Jews under Muslim rule was less oppressive.

From the eighth to the thirteenth century, most of the world's Jewish population lived under Muslim rule. They were free to practice their religion, as they were considered *dhimmis,* protected subjects or "people of the book." Their status was defined by a set of rules known as the Pact of Omar. Under these rules, their lives and property were guaranteed and the practice of religion tolerated in exchange for payment of special poll taxes called *jizya* and land taxes called *kharaj,* on condition that they behaved in a manner considered appropriate to a subject, or second-class, population. They were not allowed to build new synagogues, hold religious processions, or proselytize. They were not permitted to bear arms or ride horses, and were required to wear distinguishing clothing. Jews were forbidden to build homes higher than Muslim homes, could not adopt Muslim names or study the

Koran, and were excluded from government service. All litigation was under Muslim law, which didn't recognize the value of an oath of a *dhimmi* versus a Muslim.

Islam fell less heavily on the Jews than other faiths living under Muslim rule. Because Muslims excluded all images of worship, Christians offended them with their display of icons and crucifixes, whereas the Jews kept a lower profile and were also averse to images. For Christians and Zoroastrians under Muslim rule, putting up with these restrictions and having to pay for the privilege was degrading, and some converted. However, for Jews who had lived under Christian regimes, where the practice of their religion was forbidden and their rights were greatly restricted, the Pact of Omar was actually a relief because it recognized their status and guaranteed their right to live and worship as they pleased. And they were free to travel and reside everywhere in the world of Islam, except the Arabian peninsula.

With the establishment of the powerful Islamic Empire, the focus of Western history shifted from the Greek- and Latin-speaking world to the Arabic-speaking domain. Islam created a vast, powerful, and prosperous empire unified by the Arabic language and religion of Islam. Many of its territories formerly belonged to the Roman and Byzantine Empires, in addition to territories from the Persian Empire and elsewhere. Because agricultural taxes were so high, Jews were encouraged to move away from rural environments to the cities, where they thrived as merchants, traders, and craftsmen. They grew in power and prosperity. Islamic culture and civilization pervaded their lives. Baghdad became a powerful center, and the Jewish community of Iraq, known as the Babylonian community, was its intellectual locus. The academic leaders became the most respected authorities in matters of religious law and practice. They were called *geonim,* from the Hebrew word *gaon,* meaning "splendor." It was a time of intellectual ferment. A growing class of cosmopolitan intellectuals embraced a common heritage of philosophy and science. Great books from the ancient languages were translated into Arabic. Rabbinical scholars such as Saadia ben Joseph wrote books in Arabic on Jewish law and religion and translated the Bible into Arabic as well, along with extensive commentary. Not just scholars but all Jews adopted Arabic as their first language. Hebrew remained the language of prayer, but Arabic was used for all other philosophical writings. In everyday life, a dialect of Arabic developed, written in Hebrew characters, called Judeo-Arabic, which combined some Hebrew and Aramaic words along with a predominantly Arabic vocabulary.

By the tenth century, the Islamic Empire started to fragment into regional Islamic domains. Iraq lost its dominant position, and the Jewish community of Iraq also gradually declined in relative importance to other diaspora communities. Some Iraqi Jews emigrated to Syria, Egypt, Persia, and the Far East. During this same period, the Jewish community of

Spain flourished under Islam. Merchant scholars and courtier-rabbis held positions of power and influence in public life and took responsibility for Jewish communal affairs. This period was called the time of *convivencia,* harmony between Muslims, Christians, and Jews. (For a more thorough history of the lives of the Jews in Spain, I refer you to *Sephardic Flavors.*) In 1146, however, the fanatical Almohades, an extremist Islamic sect, took control in Spain and outlawed both Judaism and Christianity. While it wasn't the end of Jewish life there, it was a warning of what could happen to the Jews. Some families took it as an omen of things to come and left Spain. One of the families who fled Cordoba was that of a judge named Maimon, whose son, known today as Maimonides, would become the most famous Jew of the Islamic age. The family left Spain, went to Morocco and then Palestine, and eventually settled in Egypt.

Egypt had long been a center of Jewish life. Under the moderate rule of the Islamic Fatimids, who also controlled Palestine, the Jews thrived. The Jewish community in the age of Maimonides is the best documented of all medieval Jewish communities because of the survival and discovery of a *geniza,* or storage room, in one of its synagogues. Because it is considered a sacrilege in the Jewish religion to destroy any document in which the name of God appears, documents are either buried or kept in special storage chambers in synagogues. In 1897, a *geniza* was discovered and opened in the Ben Ezra synagogue in the Cairo suburb of Fustat. Its contents captured the attention of European book collectors because it was a treasure chest of documents that revealed the life and culture of the community. It not only held religious writings but also personal and business letters, commercial contracts, bills of sale and lading, marriage contracts, book lists, and inventories. These gave a fascinating insight into the everyday life of medieval Egypt from the tenth to the thirteenth century, not only of Jews but of Muslims, too.

In 1165, when Maimonides arrived in Egypt, it was under the control of the Ayyubid dynasty headed by the famed Saladin. Maimonides, a foreigner, had to overcome the opposition of local Jewish leaders in order to achieve a position of respect and authority in the community. Eventually, he was recognized as Egypt's prime rabbinic authority and became a figure of international stature whose opinion was sought from all over the Mediterranean world. His reputation rested not only in religious law but also in philosophy, science, and medicine. His most famous works were a code of Jewish Law written in Hebrew, and a philosophic treatise called *Guide to the Perplexed,* written in Arabic. He became personal physician to one of Saladin's viziers, continuing the lengthy tradition of Jewish physicians in the Muslim court.

In 1099, when the Christian Crusaders arrived in the Holy Land, Muslim dominance began to erode. The Crusades marked the start of a long and gradual process of deterioration of power that would bring the Jews changes for the worse. As the Muslims were being driven out of Spain, the coast of North Africa was under constant attack by Europeans and the Mongols had begun their march across Asia. In 1258, Baghdad fell to the Mongols, putting an end to the expansion hopes of the Islamic Empire. The balance of power was shifting in favor of Christian Europe. Islam reacted by turning on its non-Muslim subjects, the *dhimmis*. Synagogues were vandalized, Jewish doctors could no longer treat Muslim patients, and dress codes were enforced. Jews and Christians were harassed and humiliated, and often subjected to mob violence. During the fourteenth and fifteenth centuries, Islamic economic prosperity faded and power declined; living conditions for *dhimmis* deteriorated so badly that many converted to Islam to survive, or left. By 1481, Alexandria, once a center of Jewish life, had only sixty Jewish families remaining. As the Turks and Circassian Mameluk rulers took control of Egypt from 1250 to 1517, the climate became even more hostile for Jews and Christians, and they were systematically excluded from civic and public life.

Morocco was once home to the largest Jewish community in the Muslim world. Jews had settled in Morocco since the fall of the second temple in B.C.E. 150. These Jews were called the *toshavim*. As *dhimmis,* they were a protected minority when Islam swept across North Africa in the seventh century. Some were Judeo-Arabs, while others were Judeo-Berbers, known as *pilichtim,* because they claimed to be descendants of Palestinians of ancient times. The latter lived in the rural areas of the Rif and Atlas Mountains. Fundamentalist movements, however, such as that of the Almoravides and later the Almohades, attempted to force conversion on them. The Jews were segregated into separate sections of the cities in which they lived, and in general they were treated poorly. They paid extra taxes and worked at jobs disdained by Muslims, such as money lending and making jewelry. Despite this, Jews gained wealth and power. Because of their strong traditions of rabbinical scholarship, they were active in university centers such as Fez. They found careers in diplomacy and commerce and were closely linked with international economic networks. For nearly two centuries, Essaouira (Mogador) was the primary commercial center of exchange between Morocco and Europe. Jews made up 30 to 40 percent of the town's population.

Morocco had always been a refuge for the Jews of Spain during bad times, such as the late seventh century when the Visigoths ordered the Jews to convert or leave the peninsula, and in 1148 when they fled the persecution of the Almohades. (That's when Maimonides's father moved the family from Cordoba to Fez.) After the riots of 1391, many Jews had fled to Morocco and other parts of North Africa, such as Oran in Algeria and Kairouan and Djerba in Tunisia. So it was inevitable that after the Edict of Expulsion in 1492 many Sephardic Jews would look to North Africa for refuge. After all, established Portuguese and Spanish Jewish communities were already there from earlier migrations.

The Spanish Jews and Marranos from Portugal were called *megorashim* (exiles) and were on a higher cultural level than the native Jews in North Africa. They formed separate communities and settled in Tetouan, Tangier, Larache, Ceuta, and Mellila. Later, they settled in Gibraltar, which had become an English colony in 1713. In Gibraltar, the Jews could live more freely, as at that time they were allowed complete religious freedom in England and all the English colonies. They kept close ties to their relatives in England and Holland and dominated trade in textiles, fur, rubber, and beeswax. Because of their experience in Europe, they became interpreters, consular officials, and advisors to the rulers of Morocco. In 1662–1684, there was a huge influx of Jews into Tangier as that city was under English rule at that time. The *toshavim* remained in Fez and Marrakech and were still treated as second-class citizens, while Jews in Tangier were in positions of power and prestige.

In North Africa, once the fanaticism of the Almohades had died down, the discriminatory rules were applied with less rigor. The communities of what are now Tunisia and Algeria were stable and were even invigorated by the influx of Jews coming from Spain. The immigration of Spanish Jews had a favorable effect on Jewish life in Morocco as well. The Merinid dynasty, which ruled Fez from 1286 to 1465, was more tolerant of *dhimmis* than were their Muslim subjects, who were hostile to the Jews. In 1438, after a massacre that occurred because Jews were accused of putting wine in the mosques, a special Jewish quarter called the *mellah* was set aside for the Jews of Fez to protect them from riots. This pattern of ghettoization repeated itself throughout Morocco, with the result that the Jews were progressively segregated from the population at large.

Except for the period of Almohade rule, Tunisian Jews lived under relatively tolerant conditions. They lived in separate quarters called *haras* and controlled much of the trade and commerce of the country. They were merchants, interpreters, diplomats, and government officials. During the age of the enlightened Aghabid emirs in the tenth and eleventh centuries, Kairouan, the capital, became a center of Islamic and Jewish learning, supplanting Babylonia as the center of Jewish intellectual life. Most of the Jews in Tunisia were Sephardim, but Jews from the island of Djerba were a unique community with mysterious origins. They may have come from Palestine, arriving after the fall of the first temple in B.C.E. 70. Considered to be the most pious and traditional of Tunisian Jewry, they lived in separate villages and did not use Arabic script. Their dialect was laced with Hebrew and almost incomprehensible to the local Berber population. More Jews settled in Djerba after the expulsion from Spain. The two Jewish villages in Djerba are Hara Kebira and Hara Seghira; in the latter village is El Ghriba, the oldest synagogue in continuous existence in the world. It drew pilgrims from all over North Africa. In the sixteenth century, a small group of Italian Jews of Marrano origin from Livorno came to Tunisia to arrange the release of Jewish prisoners taken hostage by pirates. Many stayed, and many more emigrated from Livorno. In the nineteenth century, Italian Jews settled in the village of Hara Kebira. They did not intermarry with the native Jews, spoke Italian, and sent their children to school in Italy. They kept their own traditions and cuisine, which is a mixture of Italian, Tunisian, and Portuguese.

The second half of the fifteenth century completed the process of change in the Middle East and in Jewish history that had begun with the Crusades. A new force, the Ottoman Turks, appeared on the scene, sweeping away the old regimes and replacing them with a new and vigorous Islamic state. After progressing through Asia Minor, the Ottomans conquered the Byzantine city of Constantinople in 1453. They conquered Palestine and Egypt in 1517 and soon took over Iraq and most of North Africa. By this time, the Jews had been expelled from Spain and most of Western Europe. The rise of the Ottoman Empire presented new opportunities and a better life for the Jews in this newly ascendant world of Islam.

In *Sephardic Flavors* I related the history of the Jews under the Ottoman Empire in great detail. Jewish exiles were welcomed by Sultan Beyazit and were considered valuable additions in the expanding nation, with freedom to worship as they liked. The Sephardim, or Spanish Jewish exiles, soon came to dominate the existing Jewish communities of the Ottoman Empire. Important centers were Constantinople (now called Istanbul), Salonika, Edirne, and Smyrna. Spanish language dominated in the affairs of the Jewish community, and a new dialect called Ladino was born, combining Spanish mixed with Greek and Turkish. Along with Istanbul, Salonika was the vital center of Jewish life and culture and remained so until World War II, when most of the Jews were sent to concentration camps by the Nazis.

In the seventeenth century, a wave of Messianic movements began a demoralization of the Jewish community that corresponded with the general economic and cultural decline of the Ottoman Empire. As the empire began to weaken, followed by loss of territory, the quality of life deteriorated for the Jews and all other minorities. In Arab countries, the Turks treated the Arabs with contempt, and in return the Arabs treated the *dhimmis* badly. Jews lost almost all legal protection. Religious meetings were no longer held in public venues but retreated to the home.

Napoleon's invasion of Egypt in 1798 began a period of European intervention in the affairs of the Ottoman Empire, which gradually became what we now think of as the Middle East. In 1856, full citizenship was granted to all non-Muslims. With the relaxation of the Ottoman hold on North Africa, changes occurred within its large Jewish communities. In 1830, France occupied Algeria and soon established protectorates over Tunisia and Morocco.

Eventually, France absorbed Algeria and by 1870 granted French citizenship to the Jews. Tunisia, under somewhat Westernized Muslim rulers, retained a reasonably liberal policy toward the Jews, but because of resistance from the Muslim population, the Jews continued to live as a religious community rather than as citizens. Most Jews would have preferred French rather than Tunisian citizenship, but this didn't happen until after World War I. In Morocco, the mistreatment of the Jews was so virulent that it attracted the attention of Western Europe. A delegation was sent to Morocco, and the sultan promised that life would improve for the Jews; after the delegation departed, however, he withdrew his promise. When the French declared Morocco a protectorate, Jews were massacred in Fez in response. Moroccan Jews never did receive French citizenship, but under the protectorate their conditions gradually improved. They were no longer required to pay the *dhimmi* tax and were allowed out of the ghetto.

Egypt was officially an autonomous province of the empire, but under the rule of the pashas in the nineteenth century it behaved rather independently. The physical security and well-being of the Jews improved along with that of the country in general. Egypt modernized more rapidly than most of its neighbors, but Jews didn't receive full civic equality in Egypt until 1882, after the British occupation. In Syria, there were extreme tensions between all religious communities. The Syrian Christians hated the Jews as much as the Muslims, and it was they who brought European anti-Semitism to the Arab regions. In 1840, the first blood-libel event occurred, called the Damascus Affair. A Jewish barber was accused of killing a monk to use his blood for Passover rituals. Jewish leaders were imprisoned. There were riots in Rhodes, Beirut, and Smyrna as Muslims joined Christians in attacking the Jews. The French consul supported the accusation. Syrian Jews appealed to Jewish communities abroad for help. England intervened on behalf of the Jews, sending Moses Montefiore, a wealthy British Sephardic philanthropist, to plead the case, and eventually the sultan denounced the blood libel. In Iraq, conditions for the Jews were so bad that wealthy Baghdad families fled to India and Australia. In Iran, the Shiite form of Islam was unfavorable to the Jews, and this hostility continues to this day.

During the nineteenth century, the Jews of the Middle East became progressively more and more Westernized. This modernization was hastened by the Alliance Israelite Universelle, an organization established in Paris in 1860 to work for the emancipation, welfare, and improvement of Jews worldwide, especially in the French-held territories of the Middle East. It established a series of schools for religious and secular education throughout the Ottoman Empire and North Africa, as well as an agricultural school in Palestine. These schools were successful in producing a class of Westernized and prosperous Middle Eastern Jews. While their legal status and economic status improved, their relations with the Muslim population deteriorated, as the Muslims resented the prosperity and success of the Jews.

During the First World War, the Jews of Algeria who were French citizens fought hard for their country, but the Tunisian Jews who were not French citizens were not inclined to fight, especially in the face of the anti-Semitism of the French officials in Tunisia. Palestinian and British Jews—with the reluctant support of the British authorities— organized the Jewish Legion to help England fight the Turks. World War I marked the end of what was left of the Ottoman Empire, which by 1923 was reduced to just Anatolia or Turkey. In 1923, Turkey gave all of her citizens, including the Jews, equal rights and religious freedom. The Jews of other Middle Eastern countries were not so lucky. While most of those countries came under control of European powers, the negative patterns and tensions continued. Growing Arab nationalism put the Jews of the Middle East in an increasingly difficult position. The Arabs envisioned their countries as states free of European influences where citizenship would be based on Arab identity and Islamic religions. Jews knew this was a threat to their existence, and while some non-Zionist Jews tried to fit in as Arabic Jews, this position proved a failure. When the British occupied Iraq in World War I, the Jews and Christians begged the British to grant them British citizenship. During this brief period, Jews could serve in civil service. However, after Iraq gained its independence in 1932 it became impossible for non-Muslims to serve in government and civil service. In Egypt, which was more Westernized and cosmopolitan, Jews did participate in public life, but they realized that their future lay with the Western powers rather than with the Arab states. Radical Westernization came most naturally to the Algerian Jews, whose legal status as French citizens permitted them to identify themselves with the French and to seek assimilation. However, in France, most non-Jews didn't accept them fully.

After World War I, many Middle Eastern Jews emigrated to Western Europe and the United States. Those that didn't leave found hope and purpose in Zionism. This movement aimed at the reconstitution of the Jewish people as a nation-state and the establishment of Palestine as their homeland. Sephardic Jews felt a natural kinship with the Jews in Palestine and had been settling there gradually. After World War I, Egyptian Jews founded a number of Zionist organizations. Moroccan Jews, less Westernized and more traditionally religious, embraced the notion; however, they were opposed by the Alliance Israelite Universelle and European Zionists who failed to realize the true situation of the Jews in the Middle East. Algerian Jewry was unreceptive because they had adopted a French national identity and saw no need to emigrate. Tunisians, Syrians, and Lebanese supported the Zionist movement.

In 1929, tensions over Zionism became severe when a riot in Jerusalem brought the Palestinian nationalist movement to the attention of the Arab nations; it led to wild accusations against the Palestinian Jews. Arab nationalism took a sinister turn when it began to emulate European fascism. Nazi Germany was an appealing model to the Arabs because of its hostility to England and France, the chief colonial powers active in the Middle East. European fascism carried with it a horrible wave of anti-Semitism, incorporating the traditional Christian demonizations of the Jews and fostering the myth of an international conspiracy to bring the world under Jewish control. By the late 1930s, Hitler's *Mein Kampf* and the anti-Semitic classic *Protocols of the Elders of Zion* had been translated into Arabic, and life for the Jews in the Middle East had become untenable. In the hope of neutralizing the situation, Jewish community leaders disavowed Zionism and tried to promote Egypt as a model of peaceful Jewish-Arab cooperation. But it was too late. The German invasion of the Balkans and Greece during World War II put an end to Jewish life there. The Jewish communities of Egypt and Yemen remained relatively unharmed. But the Iraqi Jews faced a massacre in 1941 that woke them up to the realization that they had to leave.

In North Africa, the Tunisian Jews came under direct German control but the occupation was brief. Despite a history of French anti-Semitism in Algeria and the discrimination Jews felt in Morocco, they knew that their interests were with the Allied forces. The fall of France in 1940 was a terrible blow to their hopes. Algeria and Morocco came under the Vichy government led by Petain. The Jews were stripped of their French citizenship, and the anti-Jewish laws were strictly applied against all Jews in North Africa, but not pursued with such zeal in Syria and Lebanon. The sultan of Morocco declared that he was opposed to the anti-Jewish legislation and appealed to the French authorities on behalf of the Moroccan Jews. World War II convinced the Jews that it was hopeless to try to remain in the Middle East and to attempt to have normal relations with the Arabs. They also realized that they could not count on European nations for real support. Zionism intensified, along with Arab nationalism. There were anti-Zionist and anti-Jewish riots in Egypt, Libya, and Syria. When the United Nations voted to partition Palestine between Arabs and Jews in 1947, a new wave of violence erupted throughout the Middle East. Only Morocco was spared.

Before the successive waves of mass migrations to Israel, Europe, and America that began in 1948, there were an estimated 280,000 Jews in Morocco. They lived primarily in Casablanca, Fez, Meknes, Marrakech, Tetouan, and Sefrou. In the 1950s and 1960s, virtually all of the remaining Jewish population left, fearful of what would happen once Morocco gained independence, and emigrated to the newly formed state of Israel. Once Israel was established in 1948, the majority of North African Jews emigrated there. A few small communities of Jews remain, the largest in Morocco.

The end of Jewish life in the Arab world (except for Morocco) came with the establishment of the state of Israel in 1948. The Libyan and Yemenite Jewish communities evacuated their homelands and moved en masse to Israel. Iraqi Jews soon followed. Some Syrian Jews moved to more liberal and Westernized Lebanon; many more went to Israel. In Egypt, the poorer classes emigrated to Israel, while the wealthiest Jews moved to Europe and America. Large numbers of Moroccan Jews also moved to Israel, not because of repression but because of enthusiasm and support for the new state. Jews that remained in Turkey continued to thrive, but their numbers were greatly diminished. Would that the story ended here. But conflict in the Middle East continues. The story of the state of Israel and its Arab neighbors is one for which we long for a happy ending. We hope that the Jews and Arabs, who cook such beautiful food and share such sensual and vibrant flavors, may someday sit at the same table in harmony and break bread together.

⋮⋮⋮⋮⋮ THE RECIPES: SIGNATURE FLAVORS OF JUDEO-MAGHREBI AND JUDEO-ARABIC CUISINE

Traditional ingredients and use of spices create signature flavor profiles of each part of the Mediterranean world. The Italian Jewish palate is the most restrained of the Mediterranean Jewish world, almost austere in its seasoning. Because the Italians had, and still have for the most part, stellar raw materials, Italian Jewish cooks don't rely on exotic spices and herbs to achieve full-flavored food; instead they prefer the clean flavors of an uncomplicated cuisine. They use salt, a bit of pepper, and a few grains of nutmeg. The herb of choice is parsley. The Sephardim of Spain and Portugal, who settled in the Ottoman Empire, came with a Moorish/Arabized palate. Theirs was a more vivid spice palette that included cinnamon and allspice, cumin and paprika. Mint, dill, and bay leaves joined parsley in the herb bouquet. They ate rice, spinach, and artichokes and gradually embraced the foods of the New World: tomatoes, peppers, pumpkin, squashes, vanilla, and chocolate. They brought with them nut- and bread-thickened sauces, saffron, a love of citrus, a penchant for sweet-and-sour combinations, and a sweet tooth.

Judeo-Arabic cooks of the Southern Mediterranean share much of the Ottoman flavor profile, but add tamarind, pomegranate, and sesame to the pantry as well as dates, figs, and apricots. The Jews of North Africa play with an even fuller spice spectrum, using ginger, cumin, coriander, and cayenne, along with cinnamon and pepper and complex home-made spice mixtures. They do not rely on ready-made spice mixtures, in case small insects might have invaded the batch. (Commercial ras al hanout is not kosher because it might contain the cantharides beetle.) Fresh coriander (cilantro) joins mint, dill, and parsley in the

herb garden. Flower petals and orange-flower water and rose water add perfume and sweetness. Preserved lemons, tangy olives, and spicy harissa join dried fruits and nuts for a very complex and sensual cuisine.

Though Israel is on the Mediterranean, it is a melting pot with no pure cuisine of its own. Like the United States, its food reflects all of the immigrants who have settled there. You can find Ashkenazic dishes of Russian, German, and Polish Jews; food of the Yemenites, Ethiopians, and Moroccan Jews; Arabic food; and contemporary restaurant cuisine with chefs cooking Thai- and Japanese-inspired dishes. This book features Southern Mediterranean dishes taken from their original sources rather than from the eclectic Israeli kitchen.

I am crazy about Southern Mediterranean Jewish food. I love dishes that combine spices, fruit, and nuts with meat, fish, poultry, and vegetables, and that play with heat and lemon, sweet and hot, and sweet and sour. This is food that I cook quite often at home and served constantly at my restaurant, Square One. When shopping at markets in North Africa and the Middle East, I have noticed that their spices are much more intense than those we can buy at our supermarkets. So in many instances I have increased the spice measurements in the recipes in order to match the flavors that I remember and to get the same taste.

I have been fortunate to have wonderful recipe sources and an excellent reference library to support my palate's predilection and to nudge my taste memory. Judeo-Arabic food is most closely related to the Greek and Turkish food of Jews of the Ottoman Empire. It was a toss-up as to where to include hummus, eggplant purees, grain salads like tabbouleh, dolmas. Should they go in *Sephardic Flavors* or be saved for this book? I have done a bit of both. North African food provided the widest range of flavors, the most surprises, and the greatest amount of documentation from original sources. Of course, translating from French into English and from metrics into our own system of weights and measures occasionally requires some culinary adjustments. But that is part of the challenge and a good deal of the fun. See the bibliography in the back of the book if you'd like to read more about these marvelous cuisines.

Most of the source cookbooks were written by women, who did all of the work in the kitchen, working together as families: grandmothers, aunts and cousins, mother and daughter teams, mother-in-law and daughter-in-law teams. Neighbors, too. Thanks to Viviane Moryoussef and her mother Nina, Fortunée Hazan-Arama, Andrée Zana-Murat, Simy Danan, Helene Ganz Perez, Daisy Taieb, Maguy Kakon, Jeanne Ifergan, Jacqueline Cohen-Azuelos, Leone Jaffin, and Zette Guinaudeau for taking the time to transcribe the recipes as prepared in their homes and thus keeping these flavors and memories alive. Joelle Bahloul says, in her book *The Architecture of Memory,* where she traces her Algerian family's cuisine, "In women's memories ritual gestures and foods embody the slowing of the domestic pace and the strengthening of family ties." (Men's remembrance is more heavily oriented to the public dimension of ritual, such as the gatherings at synagogues, although the tastes and traditions of home are still important.) Everything was made by hand, the old-fashioned way. Marketing and cooking filled up their days and brought their families pleasure, treasured traditions, and long-lasting memories. Life is easier now, with refrigerators, freezers, stoves with ovens, blenders, and food processors. But what we miss today as we work in our appliance-laden modern kitchens is the joy of team effort, with lots of nimble and experienced hands gathered around the kitchen table forming intricately folded pastries, rolling grape leaves and stuffing vegetables, grinding nuts and spices, and trimming fruit for preserves while discussing the flavor balance and the news of the day. Many of these traditional pastries, sweets, and preserves are rarely made at home now and are purchased from stores, anonymous and compromised in flavor, less personal and idiosyncratic. Yes, many of these dishes are time-consuming. So if some of the more intricate recipes tempt you, ask a friend or family member to join you. It may be one of the best times you will have spent together. And it will create taste memories your family will never forget, and dishes they will want to cook again, in part to recapture the flavors but, more important in these times of constant change and trendiness, also to provide tradition at the table and to keep family spirit and heritage alive.

THE KOSHER LAWS

E. A. Al Maleh, in his introduction to *Moroccan Jewish Cookery* by Viviane Moryoussef, says, "The Jewish cuisine expresses the freedom to be Jewish in an Islamic land. Moreover everyone here knows that Muslim or Jewish holidays have always featured exchanges between the two communities. . . . It is a long tradition of hospitality, conviviality, respect, and mutual tolerance." The Jews and Muslims share many dishes, and at first glance, the recipes in this book don't appear any different from similar Arabic or North African recipes. What makes them Jewish are that they follow the laws of *kashrut,* the dietary laws that govern the kosher kitchen. The story persists that the dietary laws came about as a health measure to prevent the Jews from eating foods that were unclean and possibly disease ridden. Observing the laws may have had a fortunate outcome, such as the avoidance of trichinosis by not eating pork, but this was not the primary rationale. *Kashrut* is a ritual observance that leads to ethical behavior. The rabbis of the Talmudic period were content to refer to the words of the Bible when explaining the dietary laws; holiness is the only reason given for the adherence to the kosher laws. The rabbis believed that the secret of Jewish survival was separatism. By not mingling with others, Judaism would be preserved. The laws of the Bible were to be obeyed, not questioned. The twelfth-century philosopher Maimonides, in seeking a rationale for the dietary laws, surmised that they "train us to master our appetites, to accustom us to restrain our desires, and to avoid considering the pleasure of eating and drinking as the goal of man's existence." Those of us enamored of the world of food and wine might find it hard to accept that eating and drinking are not our *raison d'être*. For those hyper-creative souls who believe in total permissiveness in the kitchen, following the kosher laws might feel like a culinary straightjacket, but that's a contemporary culinary point of view. In fact, following the kosher laws brought about great creativity in observant Jewish cooks; they joyfully embraced the opportunity to prepare wonderful food using local ingredients, to adhere to traditional and well-loved recipes, and to stay within kosher boundaries.

The primary kosher laws are set forth in the Book of Leviticus, which lists kosher and not-kosher animals. The word *kosher* (derived from *kasher*) originally did not refer to food. It means "good" and "proper" and was also used to refer to ritual objects. Foods that are not kosher are considered *terayfa,* or as the word is more commonly pronounced, "treyf." Only animals with split hooves and who chew their cud are kosher. Animals with split hooves killed by hunting, and animals not killed in the ritual manner, that is, slaughtered by a *shochet,* are also forbidden. The *shochet,* or trained ritual butcher, must sever the jugular vein in one clean cut and drain all of the blood from the animal, as blood is the essence and symbol of life. To further remove all signs of blood the meat must be salted and soaked, unless the meat is to be broiled or grilled. Liver cannot be drained of blood, so it must be broiled. Only after broiling can it can be sautéed. Meats can be frozen only after koshering. Before eating the hindquarter of animal, the sciatic nerve and blood vessels attached to it must be removed. This law refers to the biblical event in Genesis when Jacob wrestled with the angel and became lame. Expert butchers can remove the nerve, but it's a time-consuming process and many kosher butchers don't handle the hindquarters of animals, selling this part to non-kosher butchers. Now you know why there are so few recipes for steak or leg of lamb. In Israel today, more butchers are learning how to remove this vein, thus broadening the kosher culinary repertoire.

A kosher fowl is a domesticated bird such as chicken, turkey, game hen, squab, duck, or goose. Only eggs from kosher birds may be eaten. Only fish with scales and fins are permitted. All shellfish, according to the book of Deuteronomy, are non-kosher. Some fish have fins and scales but lose them at some point in their development. So fish such as swordfish and sturgeon are controversial, and not all authorities permit their use. Monkfish and eel have no scales at any point in their development and so are not permitted. A fish does not have to be slaughtered in a prescribed manner, as it simply dies a natural death out of the water.

Glatt kosher is a more restrictive category of kosher used by Orthodox Jews. But the original concept has become distorted. The term *glatt* originally referred only to animal foods and meant "smooth"; that is, the lungs of the animal had to be smooth and not broken or perforated in any way. Today, a whole set of rules have been created under the aegis of *glatt,* probably to foster the original notion of separatism.

Foods are categorized as meat *(fleishig),* dairy *(milchig),* or *pareve,* a Yiddish word meaning "neutral"; the latter can be served at both meat and dairy meals. Fish is *pareve,* as are spices, grains, fruits, and vegetables. Jews are not permitted to eat meat and milk at the same meal, because in Deuteronomy it says thou shalt not cook a kid in its mother's milk. In fact, some cheeses are not considered kosher by the Orthodox because they are made with animal rennet. However, conservative Jews will eat those cheeses. (In John Cooper's book *Eat and Be Satisfied,* he points out that the Greek cheese called *kasseri,* or *casheri,* means "kosher.") The length of waiting time between eating meat and dairy can range from one to six hours, depending upon the orthodoxy of the community and rabbinical views. Different sets of dishes are kept for meat meals and dairy, and two sets of pots and pans. In the old days they could not even be washed in the same dishwasher, but now that water temperatures are so high and the dishes are essentially sterilized in the process, the same machine can be used, though dairy dishes and meat dishes are washed separately. Glass plates, because they are not absorbent, can be used for both meat and dairy meals.

Passover presents a whole other set of dietary laws. Any product considered *hametz,* that is, fermented, or that could cause fermentation, may not be eaten during Passover. Only unleavened products are served; matzoh replaces bread. Ashkenazic Jews will not eat any grains, such as wheat, spelt, oats, rye, or barley. Post-Talmudic authorities added rice and legumes to this list of forbidden foods. The Sephardic Jews did not accept this ruling, as rice and legumes formed the basis of their diet. So at Passover they eat rice and legumes, as well as some seeds or spices such as allspice, fennel, cumin, nutmeg, and sesame, and flavorings such as rose water or orange-flower water, which the Orthodox would avoid during that period. The repertoire of foods that are labeled kosher for Passover is growing all the time. Years ago you could not use powdered sugar during Passover because it contained cornstarch, but now it comes cornstarch free for the holidays.

: : : : : THE JEWISH HOLIDAYS AND HOLIDAY MENUS

: *the* SABBATH

The Sabbath is the Jewish day of rest and spiritual rejuvenation. It is a holy day, and according to Orthodox laws no work or business of any kind is to be permitted. It begins on Friday before sundown and ends at nightfall on Saturday evening. Joelle Bahloul says of the Sabbath in Algeria, "Sabbath time was . . . a time of intensified conviviality as dense and rich as the food that was served." The Sabbath is ushered into the home by the lighting of the candles; a blessing, or *kiddush,* is recited over the wine and the bread is blessed. The Sabbath dinner is a festive meal. Since no cooking, which is, of course, work, is permitted until sundown on Saturday, the Saturday midday meal has to be prepared before sunset on Friday. In the days when there was no refrigeration, freezers, or microwave ovens, these religious rules inspired great ingenuity. Cooks came up with creative culinary solutions. Dishes were cooked slowly over very low heat, buried in the *hamin,* or "oven," for many hours, even overnight. Thus we have the famed *d'fina* of North Africa (page 136) and *loubia* from Syria and Lebanon (page 149). Their textures are meltingly soft, flavors mellowed after long hours of cooking.

A versatile assortment of dishes were created that tasted good while warm but were also delicious at room temperature. Today, many of them would be called *mezze, kemia,* or *aadou*. Incidentally, Jews may cook on holidays other than the Sabbath, as making a fire is forbidden only on Yom Kippur.

SABBATH MENU I

SALADE *de* CAROTTES *et* CUMIN : : : MOROCCAN CARROT SALAD *with* CUMIN

THON *à la* TOMATE : : : TUNA *with* TOMATOES

SAMAK HARRAH, *or* : : : FISH *with* FRESH CORIANDER
POISSON *à la* CORIANDRE

MEGUINA *à la* CERVELLE *et au* VEAU : : : BRAIN *and* VEAL OMELET

D'FINA *and* SKHINA : : : SABBATH STEW

FRESH FRUITS

SABBATH MENU II

CHOUKCHOUKA, *or* MISHWYIA : : : ROASTED PEPPER *and* TOMATO SALAD

COUSCOUS DJERBIEN *au* POISSON : : : FISH COUSCOUS *from* DJERBA

LOUBIA, *or* LUBIYA M'SALLET : : : WHITE BEAN *and* MEAT STEW
or
CHEMS *la* AACHI, *or* BOULETTES : : : MEATBALLS *with* SAFFRON SUNSET SAUCE
de VIANDE *et* SAUCE CRÉPUSCULE

FRESH FRUITS

: ROSH HASHANAH

Rosh Hashanah is a holiday that celebrates the start of the new year. It occurs on the first two days of the month of Tishri, usually in late September or early October. It is a joyful holiday for the most part, wishing people good luck for the coming year. It culminates with the blowing of the *shofar,* or ram's horn, on Yom Kippur, the Day of Atonement, which is a fast day. Yom Kippur, the most solemn day of the year, is for seeking the forgiveness of people one may have hurt or offended during the year, so one can start the new year with a clean slate.

At Rosh Hashanah, a whole fish or lamb is often served, the head representing the head of the new year. There is an abundance of sweets to bring in a sweet new year. A list of foods found on the table at a Jewish home in Tunisia would include pomegranate—because it contains so many seeds, which are symbolic of the good deeds to be done in the new year— figs, quince, dates, and apples in honey, all representing a wish for a sweet new year. Sesame seeds are eaten so the virtures of the diners will be as numerous as the seeds; pumpkin is eaten for protection; garlic and leeks are believed to symbolically cancel all bad deeds; and spinach or beet greens are thought to keep enemies away. Some Sephardic Jews avoid eating food that is black in color because it represents mourning and this is a joyful holiday; recipes that usually have prunes and black raisins use apricots and golden raisins instead.

ROSH HASHANAH MENU I

SOPA *de* SIETE VERDURAS : : : ROSH HASHANAH SEVEN-VEGETABLE SOUP

or

SOUPE *de* COURGE ROUGE *et* : : : PUMPKIN SQUASH *and* CHICKPEA SOUP
POIS CHICHES *à la* CORIANDRE *with* FRESH CORIANDER

POISSON FARCI *aux* AMANDES : : : BAKED FISH STUFFED *with* ALMOND PASTE

COUSCOUS IMPERIAL : : : IMPERIAL COUSCOUS

or

KEFTA *de* VIANDE *au* CUMIN *et* CONFITURE : : : CUMIN-FLAVORED MEATBALLS
*d'*OIGNON *et* SAUCE *aux* TOMATES *with* ONION JAM *and* SPICY TOMATO SAUCE

or

KRA'A : : : LEBANESE STUFFED SQUASH
with APRICOT SAUCE

FRESH FRUITS

TARTE *au* CONFITURE *des* RAISINS *et* NOIX : : : RAISIN *and* WALNUT JAM TART

MENENAS, *or* MAAMOUL : : : STUFFED BUTTER COOKIES

ROSH HASHANAH MENU II

ASSORTED BESTELS : : : SMALL FILLED PASTRIES

TAGINE KEFTA *mn* HOOT, : : : TUNISIAN FISH BALL TAGINE
or BOULETTES *de* POISSON

or

POISSON SAUCE SOLEIL : : : FISH *with* GOLDEN SAUCE

POULET *aux* COINGS : : : ALGERIAN TAGINE *of* CHICKEN *with* QUINCE

T'FINA *aux* EPINARDS, *or* PKHAILA : : : TUNISIAN BEAN *and* BEEF STEW
with SPINACH ESSENCE

MEGUINA *à la* CERVELLE *et au* VEAU : : : BRAIN *and* VEAL OMELET

CIGARES *aux* AMANDES, *or* : : : ALMOND CIGARS
BRIKS *aux* AMANDES

NIGHT BEFORE YOM KIPPUR MENU

TFAIA : : : CHICKEN SOUP *with* EGGS

ESTOFADO : : : ROAST CHICKEN *with*
EGGPLANT *and* ONION CONFIT

SALADE *de* CAROTTES *et* CUMIN : : : MOROCCAN CARROT SALAD *with* CUMIN

CONFITURE *de* COINGS : : : QUINCE CONSERVE

CIGARES *aux* AMANDES, *or* : : : ALMOND CIGARS
BRIKS *aux* AMANDES

MENU TO BREAK THE FAST AFTER YOM KIPPUR

MOUNAS : : : ALGERIAN ORANGE BREAD

AJLOUK *d'*AUBERGINE : : : HAOUARI'S SPICY EGGPLANT PUREE

H'RIRA *de* KIPPOUR : : : LEMONY BEAN *and* RICE SOUP *for* YOM KIPPUR

AL BARANIYA : : : SWEET EGGPLANT
see
AUBERGINES CONFIT : : : CANDIED EGGPLANT

COUSCOUS IMPERIAL : : : IMPERIAL COUSCOUS
or
DAR LAARCH, *or* BOULETTES : : : *The* BRIDE'S CHICKEN MEATBALLS
de POULET DITES *la* MARIÉE

FRESH FRUITS

: SUKKOT

The Feast of the Tabernacles, or Sukkot, begins on the evening of the fifteenth day of the month of Tishri, which is usually in October. It lasts for seven days. *Tabernacle* is derived from the Latin word *tabernaculum,* meaning a hut, or temporary shelter. This is a harvest festival, and temporary branch- or straw-covered booths *(sukkas)* are constructed outdoors, in memory of ancestors who were forced to dwell outside in their wanderings. Four kinds of branches, which symbolize moral and ethical values of eternal faith, are carried during this holiday. They are the *etrog,* or citron; the *lulav,* or palm branch; the *hadas,* or myrtle branch; and the *aravah,* or willow branch. Simchat Torah is the last day of Sukkot; its name means "joy of the Torah," because that is the day when the annual cycle of Torah reading, the five Books of Moses, is completed.

SUKKOT MENU

ZAHLOUK, *or* SALADE *d'*AUBERGINES : : : EGGPLANT SALAD *with* PRESERVED LEMON
au CITRON CONFIT

ARTICHAUTS, FENOUILS, *et* : : : ARTICHOKES, FENNEL, *and* CELERY ROOT
CÉLERI-RAVES *au* CITRON   *with* LEMON

BESSARA, *or* BICHRA : : : FAVA *or* LENTIL SOUP

POULET FARCI *avec* COUSCOUS *aux* : : : COUSCOUS-STUFFED CHICKEN *with*
OLIVES *et* CITRONS CONFITS   OLIVES *and* PRESERVED LEMONS

B'STILLA : : : MOROCCAN CHICKEN *and* ALMOND PIE

MECHOUI : : : ROAST LAMB *with* MOROCCAN SPICES
or
KEFTA *de* VIANDE *au* CUMIN *et* CONFITURE : : : CUMIN-FLAVORED MEATBALLS
*d'*OIGNON *et* SAUCE *aux* TOMATES   *with* ONION JAM *and* SPICY TOMATO SAUCE

Le PAILLE : : : CEREMONIAL CAKE *from* MOROCCO

SIMCHAT TORAH MENU

SLATA FILFIL, *or* FEFLA : : : HAOUARI'S ROASTED PEPPER SALAD

MEGUINA *à la* CERVELLE *et au* VEAU : : : BRAIN *and* VEAL OMELET

KEFTA *de* VIANDE *au* CUMIN *et* CONFITURE : : : CUMIN-FLAVORED MEATBALLS
*d'*OIGNON *et* SAUCE *aux* TOMATES   *with* ONION JAM *and* SPICY TOMATO SAUCE

MROUZIA : : : LAMB TAGINE *with* PRUNES *and* HONEY
or
MECHOUI : : : ROAST LAMB *with* MOROCCAN SPICES

DATTES *à la* PÂTÉ *d'*AMANDES : : : DATES STUFFED *with* ALMOND PASTE
or
CIGARES *aux* AMANDES, *or* BRIKS *aux* AMANDES : : : ALMOND CIGARS

: HANUKKAH

Hanukkah is also known as the Festival of Lights. It occurs on the twenty-fifth day of Kislev, which usually falls in December, and lasts eight days. It refers to the battle in which the Macabees defeated the enemy and recaptured Jerusalem. Although the lamp in the Temple appeared as if it had enough oil for only one night, the oil burned for eight days. To celebrate this miracle, the candles of the menorah are lit for eight consecutive evenings. Fried foods are often served at this holiday, in reference to the oil. Obviously, the entire menu would not be fried, but the following are some dishes that can be served during the eight days of Hanukkah.

HANUKKAH DISHES

B'STILLA : : : MOROCCAN CHICKEN *and* ALMOND PIE

ASSORTED BRIKS : : : SAVORY *and* SWEET PASTRIES, *fried*

ASSORTED BESTELS : : : SMALL FILLED PASTRIES, *fried*

KIBBEH *bil* SINAYEH : : : BAKED LAYERED BULGUR *and* MEAT

BAZARGAN : : : SYRIAN CRACKED-WHEAT SALAD

DJEJ MACARUNI : : : SYRIAN CHICKEN *with* MACARONI

RAGOUT *d'*ARTICHAUTS FARCIS : : : STUFFED ARTICHOKE STEW

CHOUKCHOUKA *aux* OEUFS : : : ROASTED PEPPER *and* TOMATO SALAD *with* EGGS

TAGINE KEFTA *mn* HOOT, : : : TUNISIAN FISH BALL TAGINE
or BOULETTES *de* POISSON

SFENJ : : : MOROCCAN HANUKKAH DOUGHNUTS

: TU B'SHEVAT

Tu B'Shevat, the New Year of the Trees, occurs in late January or early February, the time of year in the Mediterranean when the trees are just starting their early blooming. It is also called *Las Frutas* by the Sephardim. It is celebrated by the planting of trees. At the table, it is celebrated by eating lots of winter fruits and dried summer fruits such as dates and figs.

TU B'SHEVAT MENU

MROUZIA : : : LAMB TAGINE *with* PRUNES *and* HONEY

MENENAS, *or* MAAMOUL : : : STUFFED BUTTER COOKIES

SALADE *d'*ARTICHAUTS CUIT *à l'*ORANGE : : : ARTICHOKES *cooked with* ORANGE

SALADE *d'*ORANGES : : : MOROCCAN ORANGE SALAD *with* OLIVES

DATTES *à la* PÂTÉ *d'*AMANDES : : : DATES STUFFED *with* ALMOND PASTE

: PURIM

This joyful holiday, also called the Festival of Lots, is celebrated on the fourteenth day of the month of Adar, usually in March, and commemorates the triumph of Queen Esther, aided by her cousin Mordecai, in outwitting the evil minister Haman who had advised King Ahasueros to kill all the Jews. Many dishes are sweet and sour, to recall how sweet it was to conquer adversity.

PURIM MENU

T'FINA *aux* EPINARDS, *or* PKHAILA : : : TUNISIAN BEAN *and* BEEF STEW
with SPINACH ESSENCE

B'STILLA : : : MOROCCAN CHICKEN *and* ALMOND PIE

DJEJ MACARUNI : : : SYRIAN CHICKEN *with* MACARONI

DJEJ MIHSHEE *bi* ROZ (*bi* BURGHUL) : : : ROAST CHICKEN STUFFED *with* RICE
(*or* BULGUR)

RAGOUT *d'*ARTICHAUTS FARCIS : : : STUFFED ARTICHOKE STEW

KNEGLETS, *or* KNADELS : : : MARZIPAN-FILLED COOKIES

GORAYEBAH : : : PURIM BUTTER COOKIES

Le PAILLE : : : CEREMONIAL CAKE *from* MOROCCO

MENENAS, *or* MAAMOUL : : : STUFFED BUTTER COOKIES

: PASSOVER

This holiday begins on the fourteenth day of Nissan, usually in April, and lasts eight days. It celebrates the exodus of the Jews from Egypt, which occurred in such haste that their bread dough did not have time to rise. To commemorate this event, no leavened foods *(hametz)* may be eaten. Matzoh is the main bread product served, but it is made with a special wheat flour ground just before baking so that it will not have time to ferment. Originally, matzoh were round, but in 1875 a square matzoh press was invented in England and it has been in use ever since. Joelle Bahloul in her book *The Architecture of Memory* describes the preparation of the matzoh before they went to communal ovens. "We'd make our own Passover matzoh. Each family would make six or seven kilos. We'd make them round and flat. So we'd have to help each other. We'd go down into the courtyard . . . . We'd have to wait until it rained . . . the water had to spend a night under the stars to be kosher . . . the next day we'd prepare the dough. We'd moisten it gradually, adding water, salt." Each day they'd bake a batch for one family. One woman was in charge of the dough; because it wasn't supposed to rise, she would keep it wet. Another rolled out the dough, and yet another baked it on the *kanoun* using a *tabona,* a large three-legged brazier used for making Arab flat bread.

Special china and silverware are used for Passover, and a major spring cleaning is usually undertaken to rid the house of any traces of *hametz*. Joelle Bahloul's cousin Clarisse tells of this time in their Algerian household: "For the entire month before Passover we had to clean the house. We had to take everything out of the house and put it in the courtyard. We'd clean and then gradually bring everything back in. My aunt Esther would live for a month on the balcony so she wouldn't dirty her house. Her rooms opened onto the balcony and there was a laundry room there, so during the month before Passover she'd live there."

The Passover ritual dinners called *Seders* (the word means "order") occur the first and second nights of the holiday. At the Seder, Jews recite the story of how the angel of death passed over the houses of the Jews and tell the history of the exodus, from a book called the *Haggadah*. Four glasses of wine are drunk in memory of God's four promises of freedom in Israel. The centerpiece of the table is the Seder plate, which is divided into sections to hold the ritual foods: the *karpas,* a mild green herb such as parsley or romaine, representing new growth, is dipped in saltwater that represents the tears of the slaves; the *maror,* or bitter herb, which is usually horseradish or chicory, to remember the bitter times of slavery; the *betza,* or roasted egg, symbolizes the sacrificial offering to God in the Temple, required as an expression of Thanksgiving; the *zeroah,* or roasted lamb bone, represents the Paschal sacrifice of a lamb by the slaves on the eve of the exodus and symbolizes religious freedom; and finally, the *haroset,* a fruit-and-nut paste, represents the mortar used by the Jews to construct the pyramids.

PASSOVER MENU I

MATZOH

HAROSET : : : PASSOVER FRUIT CONDIMENT

VELOUTÉ VERT *de* PESSAH : : : GREEN PUREE *for* PASSOVER

ARTICHAUTS, FENOUILS, *et* : : : ARTICHOKES, FENNEL, *and*
CÉLERI-RAVES *au* CITRON   CELERY ROOT *with* LEMON

SALADE *des* CAROTTES *et* CUMIN : : : MOROCCAN CARROT SALAD *with* CUMIN

TAGINE KEFTA *mn* HOOT, *or* : : : TUNISIAN FISH BALL TAGINE
BOULETTES *de* POISSON

D'FINA *and* SKHINA : : : SABBATH STEW

OSBANE : : : TUNISIAN SAUSAGE

FRESH *and* DRIED FRUITS

PASSOVER MENU II

MATZOH

SORDA : : : PASSOVER MATZOH SOUP

PASTEL *de* MERLAN : : : WHITING *and* POTATO PIE

MEGUINA *à la* CERVELLE *et au* VEAU : : : BRAIN *and* VEAL OMELET

MSOKI : : : TUNISIAN PASSOVER STEW
with SPRING VEGETABLES

RAGOUT *d'*ARTICHAUTS FARCIS : : : STUFFED ARTICHOKE STEW

MROUZIA : : : LAMB TAGINE *with* PRUNES *and* HONEY

ASSORTED NOUGATS

FRESH *and* STUFFED DRIED FRUITS

PASSOVER LUNCH MENU

DJIADJIA TAIRAT : : : ALGERIAN PASSOVER MATZOH
and PEA OMELET

CHOUKCHOUKA *aux* OEUFS : : : ROASTED PEPPER *and* TOMATO SALAD *with* EGGS

MARCOUDE : : : POTATO *and* EGG CAKE

: MIMOUNA, *or* MAIMOUNA

Most Jews celebrate Passover for eight days. However, in Morocco an additional day is added to the holiday, called Mimouna, sometimes spelled Maimouna. The origin of the word is debated. Some say it comes from the Hebrew Arabic *mammon,* which means "wealth," indicating a day of prosperity. Others say it is derived from the Hebrew word *emunah,* meaning "faith." Finally, some attribute it to the father of the scholar Moses Maimonides, Maimon, whose death is commemorated the day after Passover. A festival of friendship, it is characterized by visits to many homes on one night. People first go to the rabbi's house, then to their parents' homes, and then to other homes that are significant in their relationships. It is a traditional time for matchmaking. At each house there is singing, an exchange of blessings, and a sampling of a token food. Tables are set with an array of sweets, cookies, marzipan, stuffed dates, macaroons, and so on. These sweets conform to the Passover regulations, as they were prepared during the holiday. Symbols of good luck are also on the table: a bowl of fresh flour, a sheaf of new wheat, a raw whole fish, a jar of honey, pitchers of milk and wine, eggs, a crystal bowl of dates.

: SHAVOUT

Shavout is the Festival of Weeks, a culmination of the seven weeks since Passover. It celebrates the anniversary of the Revelation on Mount Sinai and the giving of the Torah, or Five Books of Moses. It falls on the sixth day of Sivan, usually in late May or early June, when it is traditional to decorate the synagogue with flowers, leaves, and tree branches. Another name for Shavout is the Festival of First Fruits, or Yom Ha-Bikkurim, because it was at this time that the first wheat crop was harvested. This is usually a dairy meal, and cheese-filled pastries are featured.

SHAVOUT MENU

BESTELS *de* FROMAGE : : : CHEESE PASTRIES

MARCOUDE : : : POTATO *and* EGG CAKE

COUSCOUS IMPERIAL : : : IMPERIAL COUSCOUS

SAMAK *bil* TAHINEH : : : FISH *with* TAHINI SAUCE

ROZ *bil* HALEEB : : : SYRIAN RICE PUDDING

FRESH FRUITS

: TISHA B'AV

This holiday falls on the ninth day of Av (mid-July to early August) and commemorates the fall of the First Temple in Jerusalem in 586 B.C. and the fall of the Second Temple in A.D. 70. From the seventeenth day of Tammuz, observant Jews enter a three-week period of mourning until Tisha B'Av. During this time, weddings are not performed, music is not played, and no new clothing may be worn. Beginning with the first day of Av, people refrain from eating meat except on the Sabbath. Vegetarian and dairy menus are served. Tisha B'Av is a fast day among the Orthodox. Symbolic foods of mourning, such as lentil soup and h'rira, are served. They are often accompanied with small cheese pastries such as *bestels de fromage.*

APPETIZERS, EGG DISHES, AND CONDIMENTS

chapter 1

APPETIZERS, EGG DISHES, AND CONDIMENTS

In North Africa and the Middle East, the meal begins with an assortment of small plates called *mezze*, also called *kemia* in Algeria or *aadu* in Tunisia. There are always some salads, a bowl of olives, and spreads such as hummus or eggplant. Warm tidbits such as falafel or *bestels* are often added to the room-temperature dishes.

While in Spain the *tortilla*, or omelet, has become an integral part of the tapas assortment, among Sephardic Jews of the Southern Mediterranean it is eaten as lunch or a light supper. It might be made more substantial with potatoes or chickpeas, or matzoh during Passover. The most festive omelet for holidays, the *meguina*, is made with brains, or sometimes brains and eggs, or sometimes brains and chicken or meat. To stretch a vegetable dish, eggs might be poached on top or scrambled in. This *egga*, or *ojja*, is occasionally enriched with *merguez*, a spicy beef sausage. The pantry is stocked with fragrant spices from the spice market, preserved lemons, and condiments such as harissa to add heat to milder dishes and to create some of the signature flavors of this vibrant cuisine.

OLIVES MARINÉES

MARINATED OLIVES

A bowl of olives is always part of the *mezze* table. Some Algerian cooks blanch the olives in boiling water. Others simply rinse the olives well. Moroccans like to cover them with a pungent marinade.

Makes about 2 cups

ALGERIAN SPICED GREEN OLIVES:

2 CUPS ($^1/_2$ POUND) GREEN OLIVES, DRAINED

3 TO 4 TABLESPOONS OLIVE OIL

3 CLOVES GARLIC, MINCED

$^1/_2$ TEASPOON SWEET PAPRIKA

PINCH OF CAYENNE PEPPER

2 TO 3 BAY LEAVES (OPTIONAL)

2 TABLESPOONS FRESH LEMON JUICE

Crack the olives with a mallet, the flat side of a cleaver, or a small, heavy saucepan. Put them in a bowl and cover with cold water. Soak overnight. Drain well.

In a sauté pan or skillet, heat the oil over low heat and cook the garlic, spices, and bay leaves, if using, for 3 minutes. Add the olives and cook for 2 to 4 minutes. Remove from heat. Add the lemon juice and let cool. Place in sterilized jars and refrigerate for at least 2 or up to 7 days.

MOROCCAN OLIVES:

2 CUPS ($^1/_2$ POUND) BRINED BLACK OR GREEN OLIVES, DRAINED

6 TABLESPOONS CHOPPED FRESH FLAT-LEAF PARSLEY

6 TABLESPOONS CHOPPED FRESH CORIANDER (CILANTRO)

3 CLOVES GARLIC, MINCED

1 TEASPOON RED PEPPER FLAKES, OR 2 FRESH HOT PEPPERS, CUT INTO SLIVERS

$^1/_2$ TEASPOON GROUND CUMIN

$^1/_2$ CUP OLIVE OIL

2 TEASPOONS FRESH LEMON JUICE

FEW STRIPS OF LEMON OR ORANGE ZEST, OR PEEL OF $^1/_2$ PRESERVED LEMON AND SOME OF ITS JUICE (PAGE 50)

Crack the olives with a mallet, the flat side of a cleaver, or a small, heavy saucepan. Put them in a bowl and cover with cold water. Soak overnight. Drain well. Toss with the remaining ingredients. Place in hot, sterilized jars and refrigerate for at least 2 or up to 7 days.

Variation: Olives Noir à l'Orange (Black Olives with Bitter Orange) Combine black olives with the chopped pulp of 2 small bitter or blood oranges. Add minced garlic, red pepper flakes, cumin, and olive oil as above. If you use sweet oranges, add lemon juice, too.

: : : : : :

OLIVES VERTS *aux* ANCHOIS

BRAISED OLIVES WITH ANCHOVIES

Most of us are used to eating olives served at room temperature, but they are totally transformed when served warm. This Algerian recipe is from Leone Jaffin's Aunt Olga.

Serves 6

2 TABLESPOONS EXTRA-VIRGIN OLIVE OIL

3 CLOVES GARLIC, MINCED

3 ANCHOVY FILLETS, CHOPPED

4 CUPS (1 POUND) GREEN OLIVES, DRAINED

$1/2$ CUP WATER

1 LEMON, PEELED AND CHOPPED

$1/2$ TEASPOON SWEET PAPRIKA

$1/2$ TEASPOON GROUND CUMIN

PINCH OF GROUND CAYENNE PEPPER

2 EGGS, LIGHTLY BEATEN (OPTIONAL)

Crack the olives with a mallet, the flat side of a cleaver, or a small, heavy saucepan. Put them in a bowl and cover with cold water. Soak overnight.

In a medium sauté pan or skillet, heat the oil over low heat. Add the garlic and anchovies and cook for a few minutes. Add the olives, water, lemon, and spices. Cook over low heat until the olives are tender, about 10 minutes. Just before serving, add the eggs if using; swirl over low heat for 2 to 3 minutes, just enough to set the eggs. Serve at once.

: : : : : :

HUMMUS

CHICKPEA PUREE

Not only is hummus a classic spread beloved in Syria, Lebanon, and Israel, but versions of it seem to appear in every supermarket refrigerator case here in the United States. It has become the perfect appetizer and probably is lunch for many a person trapped at a desk. Serve hummus with warm pita bread or spears of cucumber, radish, carrot, and green onion. It also can be a rich and creamy garnish for falafel.

Serves 6

1 CUP DRIED CHICKPEAS, SOAKED OVERNIGHT AND DRAINED

4 CUPS WATER

2 TEASPOONS SALT, PLUS MORE TO TASTE

6 TABLESPOONS TAHINI (SESAME PASTE)

2 LARGE CLOVES GARLIC, ANY GREEN SPROUTS REMOVED, MINCED

$1/2$ CUP FRESH LEMON JUICE, OR TO TASTE

PINCH OF CAYENNE PEPPER, OR TO TASTE

1 TEASPOON GROUND CUMIN (OPTIONAL)

2 TABLESPOONS EXTRA-VIRGIN OLIVE OIL

SWEET PAPRIKA TO TASTE

3 TABLESPOONS CHOPPED FRESH FLAT-LEAF PARSLEY

2 TABLESPOONS PINE NUTS, TOASTED

PITA BREAD, WARMED

Put the chickpeas in a 2-quart soup pot, add the water, and bring to a boil. Reduce heat, cover, and simmer until very soft, about 1 hour or more. Add the 2 teaspoons salt after 30 minutes. Drain the chickpeas, reserving the cooking liquid, and transfer them to a food processor. Pulse to puree. Add the tahini, garlic, lemon juice, cayenne, and cumin, if using, and puree again.

Pulse in enough cold water to achieve a spreadable consistency and season with salt to taste. If you are serving it right away, spoon the hummus onto a shallow plate and smooth it with a spoon or spatula. Sprinkle with the olive oil, paprika, parsley, and toasted pine nuts. Serve with the pita bread. If you make the hummus hours in advance, the mixture will thicken as it stands, so you will need to thin it with the reserved cooking liquid to regain the proper consistency.

: : : : : :

FALAFEL

CHICKPEA CROQUETTES

Andalusía was known for its many shops specializing in fried foods. The Sephardic passion for fried foods spread to the Italian Jews, who love a good *fritto misto,* and to the Middle East as well. Falafel exemplify the Sephardic fritter tradition at its best. These crunchy chickpea croquettes are Egyptian in origin but are now equally popular in Syria and Lebanon, and have become a signature dish of Israel. The crunchy fried falafel are tucked into warm pita bread with chopped tomato, cucumber, and tahini dressing, possibly enriched by a dollop of hummus. Instead of using bread and flour to bind the mixture, some cooks add $1/2$ cup soaked bulgur. Others don't cook the chickpeas, but merely soak them. I think falafel are better with cooked chickpeas, but you don't have to cook them for a long time. And, yes, you may use canned chickpeas, though the texture will be softer.

Makes 16 *falafel*

1 CUP DRIED CHICKPEAS, SOAKED OVERNIGHT AND
　　DRAINED
4 CUPS WATER
2 TEASPOONS SALT, PLUS MORE TO TASTE
1 THICK SLICE RUSTIC WHITE BREAD, CRUST REMOVED
2 TABLESPOONS FLOUR, PLUS ABOUT 1 CUP
　　FOR COATING
$1/2$ TEASPOON BAKING SODA
3 CLOVES GARLIC, MINCED
1 EGG
2 TABLESPOONS CHOPPED FRESH FLAT-LEAF PARSLEY
$1/2$ TEASPOON FRESHLY GROUND BLACK PEPPER
$1/2$ TEASPOON CAYENNE PEPPER
1 TEASPOON GROUND CUMIN
$1/2$ TEASPOON GROUND TURMERIC
$1/2$ TEASPOON GROUND CORIANDER

CANOLA OR VEGETABLE OIL FOR DEEP-FRYING
PITA BREADS, HEATED
2 TOMATOES, CHOPPED
1 CUCUMBER, CHOPPED
TAHINYEH (PAGE 42)
HUMMUS (PAGE 39), OPTIONAL

Put the chickpeas in a 2-quart soup pot, add the water, and bring to a boil. Reduce heat, cover, and simmer for 25 to 30 minutes. Add the 2 teaspoons salt after 20 minutes of cooking. Drain the chickpeas and reserve the liquid. Grind the chickpeas through the coarse blade of a meat grinder or pulse in a food processor. Add the bread, the 2 tablespoons flour, the baking soda, garlic, egg, and seasonings and mix well. Add salt to taste. Form into 1-inch balls, then flatten each slightly in your hand.

In a deep saucepan or a wok, heat 3 inches of oil to 375 degrees F. Dip the falafel into flour and deep-fry in batches until golden. Using a skimmer, transfer to paper towels to drain. Tuck into warm pita bread, along with about 2 tablespoons *each* chopped tomatoes and cucumber, and a generous drizzle of tahini dressing and some hummus, if using.

TAHINYEH|**TAHINI DRESSING**

Makes about 2 cups

1/2 CUP TAHINI (SESAME PASTE)

1/2 CUP FRESH LEMON JUICE

1 CUP WATER

2 LARGE CLOVES GARLIC, ANY GREEN SPROUTS
    REMOVED, MINCED

SALT TO TASTE

PINCH OF CAYENNE PEPPER OR FRESHLY GROUND
    BLACK PEPPER TO TASTE

WATER AS NEEDED

In a food processor, combine all the ingredients
except the water and puree. Add water to achieve
the consistency for salad dressing, or less to make
a spreadable dip.

: : : : : :

MERTZEL

CHICKPEA OMELET WITH CHICKEN

Moroccan families serve this hearty omelet to break
the Yom Kippur fast. Mertzel resembles a Spanish
potato *tortilla,* but is made with chickpeas instead
of potatoes. It is part of an old Sephardic omelet
tradition that includes the Algerian *meguina,* made
with vegetables, chicken, and eggs; the *marcoude* of
Tunisia; and the *almodrotes, fritadas,* and *quajados* of
the Greek and Turkish Jews. This version is a combination of recipes from *La table juive* and *La cuisine
juive d'Afrique du Nord.*

Serves 6

1 CUP DRIED CHICKPEAS, SOAKED OVERNIGHT AND
    DRAINED

4 CUPS WATER

3 TABLESPOONS OLIVE OIL, PLUS MORE FOR DRIZZLING

1/2 TEASPOON SWEET PAPRIKA

2 CLOVES GARLIC, MINCED

1 TEASPOON SALT

FRESHLY GROUND PEPPER TO TASTE

8 EGGS

1 BONELESS, SKINLESS WHOLE CHICKEN BREAST,
    COOKED AND DICED OR SHREDDED

FRESHLY GRATED NUTMEG (OPTIONAL)

PINCH OF CRUSHED SAFFRON THREADS (OPTIONAL)

Put the chickpeas in a 2-quart soup pot, add the
water, and bring to a boil. Reduce heat, cover, and
simmer for about 30 minutes, or until almost tender.

In a nonstick medium sauté pan or skillet, heat the
3 tablespoons oil over low heat. Add the paprika,
garlic, salt, pepper, and the chickpeas and their
cooking liquid. Simmer for 30 minutes, adding a bit
of water if the mixture is too dry.

Add the eggs, chicken, and nutmeg and/or saffron,
if using. Mix well and drizzle with oil. Cover, reduce
heat to low, and cook until the eggs are set and the
sides are golden, about 30 minutes. Unmold onto a
serving plate. Serve warm.

Variation: Some versions of this dish use
more chicken and half the number of eggs; the mixture
is layered in a casserole and baked until set.

: : : : : :

MEGUINA *à la* CERVELLE *et au* VEAU

BRAIN AND VEAL OMELET

To those wary of innards, it will no doubt come as a huge surprise that a brain-and-hard-cooked-egg omelet is a signature dish of North African Jews and is served on festive occasions and holidays. It's called *meguina* in Algeria and Morocco, *menina* in Tunisia. Both Tunisian and Moroccan Jews make *meguina* with chicken and brains, minus the onions, peas, and carrots, sometimes adding potatoes. Some versions are just brains and eggs. The brains are precooked and cut into small pieces that are folded into the beaten egg mixture, or they may be arranged between layers of egg and meat mixture. This recipe adds veal to the mix and is adapted from Leone Jaffin's *150 recettes et mille et un souvenirs d'une juive d'Algérie*. The squeamish can leave out the brains and just use the veal and eggs, but really, it's worth a try in the original manner.

Serves 10

1 CALF'S BRAIN

1 TABLESPOON WHITE WINE VINEGAR

1/2 POUND STEWING VEAL, CUT INTO 1/3-INCH DICE

3 LARGE CARROTS, CUT IN 1/3-INCH ROUNDS

1/2 POUND GREEN PEAS, SHELLED (ABOUT 1/2 CUP)

2 TABLESPOONS PEANUT OIL

2 ONIONS, FINELY CHOPPED

12 EGGS

SALT AND FRESHLY GROUND BLACK PEPPER TO TASTE

2 LEMONS, CUT INTO WEDGES

Soak the brain in cold water with the vinegar for about 30 minutes. Carefully remove the membrane under cold water. In a large saucepan, blanch the brain in salted boiling water for 3 minutes. Using a skimmer, transfer the brain to paper towels to drain, then cut into large dice.

Preheat the oven to 375 degrees F. Return the salted water to a boil and cook the diced veal and the carrots for 10 minutes. Add the peas and simmer for 5 minutes. Drain the veal and vegetables and return to the pan.

In a sauté pan or skillet, heat the oil over low heat and cook the onions until golden, about 15 minutes. Add to the veal mixture.

Cook 3 of the eggs in boiling water for 9 minutes. Drain and let cool in cold water. Peel. Beat the remaining 9 eggs, season with salt and pepper, and add to the veal mixture. Carefully fold in the brain. Oil a 9-by-5-inch Pyrex loaf dish and heat it in the oven. Carefully remove it and spoon in half the veal mixture, then the hard-cooked eggs nestled lengthwise in a line down the middle, then the rest of the veal. Bake until set and golden, about 1 hour. Let cool in the dish. Unmold and slice. Serve with the lemon wedges.

Note: You can substitute chicken for the veal.

: : : : : :

DJIADJIA TAIRAT ★ ALGERIAN PASSOVER MATZOH AND PEA OMELET

OJJA *bil* MERGUEZ

TUNISIAN OMELET WITH SAUSAGE, POTATOES, AND PEPPERS

The difference between an *ojja* (or *egga,* as it is sometimes called) and a *chakchouka* is that in an *ojja* the eggs are beaten and stirred into the filling like a frittata, as opposed to being cooked on top. *Chakchouka* is not to be confused with *choukchouka,* the Algerian name for a salad of roasted peppers and tomatoes, also known as *mishwiya* in Morocco and Tunisia.

Serves 6 TO 8

1/4 CUP OLIVE OIL

1 POUND MERGUEZ SAUSAGE (PAGE 150), CUT INTO
    1-INCH PIECES

3 GREEN BELL PEPPERS, SEEDED, DERIBBED, AND CUT
    INTO 1/4-INCH STRIPS

3 CLOVES GARLIC, MINCED

1/2 TEASPOON HARISSA (PAGE 48), DISSOLVED IN
    2 TABLESPOONS WATER

1 TEASPOON GROUND CARAWAY SEEDS

2 TEASPOONS SWEET PAPRIKA

1/4 CUP WATER

3 TOMATOES, PEELED, SEEDED, AND COARSELY
    CHOPPED

4 BOILING POTATOES, COOKED, AND PEELED,
    AND CUBED

9 EGGS, BEATEN

SALT AND FRESHLY GROUND BLACK PEPPER TO TASTE

In a large sauté pan or skillet, heat the oil over high heat. Add the merguez and fry, turning once, until browned on both sides. Add the bell peppers and garlic and cook for 5 minutes, stirring often. Reduce heat and add the harissa, caraway, paprika, water, tomatoes, and potatoes. Simmer until thickened, about 15 minutes.

Add the eggs to the sausage mixture, stirring until the eggs have thickened and are creamy. Sprinkle with salt and pepper and serve at once.

: : : : : :

DJIADJIA TAIRAT

ALGERIAN PASSOVER MATZOH AND PEA OMELET

Leone Jaffin's Aunt Colette gave her this recipe for a Passover omelet. Instead of cooking the omelet in oil, she uses meat drippings; you can use chicken fat as well. The addition of garlic and hot pepper makes this a very lively version of *matzoh brei.*

Serves 4

5 TABLESPOONS MEAT DRIPPINGS, CHICKEN FAT, OR
    PEANUT OIL

6 TO 8 CLOVES GARLIC, COARSELY CHOPPED

2 CUPS WATER

SALT AND FRESHLY GROUND BLACK PEPPER TO TASTE

1 BAY LEAF

1 TEASPOON SWEET PAPRIKA

1 SMALL DRIED RED PEPPER, CRUSHED, OR 1/2 TEASPOON
    RED PEPPER FLAKES

1 TEASPOON GROUND CARAWAY OR CUMIN

4 MATZOH, BROKEN INTO SMALL PIECES

1 POUND GREEN PEAS, SHELLED AND BLANCHED
    (ABOUT 1 CUP)

6 EGGS, BEATEN

In a sauté pan or skillet, heat the drippings, fat, or oil over medium heat. Add the garlic and sauté for 2 minutes. Add the water, salt, pepper, bay leaf, paprika, red pepper, and caraway or cumin. When the liquid boils, add the matzoh and peas. Cook until most of the water is absorbed, about 10 minutes.

MARCOUDE ★ **POTATO AND EGG CAKE**

Pour the eggs over the matzoh. Using a fork, pull the sides of the omelet in so the rest of the eggs can run underneath. When the omelet is set but still quite moist, loosen the sides with a spatula, slide it onto a plate, and serve at once.

: : : : : :

MARCOUDE
POTATO AND EGG CAKE

Marcoude is a North African Sephardic version of the Spanish potato *tortilla.* This dish is called *cuajada* in *La table juive,* based on an Arabic term for *qas'ah,* a Spanish cooking vessel such as a *cazuela.* This Algerian recipe comes from Leone Jaffin. The recipe calls for russets, as opposed to the new potatoes that Simy Danan uses in *La nouvelle cuisine judeo-marocaine* (see variation). If you use only half the eggs, it becomes a potato gratin or potato cake.

Serves 8 as a side dish, 4 as a main dish

2 1/2 POUNDS RUSSET POTATOES, PEELED AND
    CUT INTO PIECES
4 TO 6 CLOVES GARLIC
8 EGGS, LIGHTLY BEATEN
3 LARGE GREEN ONIONS, INCLUDING TENDER GREEN
    PARTS, MINCED
3 TABLESPOONS CHOPPED FRESH FLAT-LEAF PARSLEY
SALT AND FRESHLY GROUND BLACK PEPPER TO TASTE
FRESHLY GRATED NUTMEG TO TASTE

Cook the potatoes and garlic in salted boiling water until the potatoes are soft, about 20 minutes. Drain and mash with a fork. Stir in the eggs, green onions, parsley, salt, pepper, and nutmeg. Mix well.

Preheat the oven to 400 degrees F. Oil a 10-inch round pie dish or gratin dish and heat it in the oven. Spread the potato mixture in the dish. Bake until golden, about 30 minutes. Serve hot or warm.

Variation: Simy Danan's Soufflé de Pommes de Terre (Potato Cake from Fez) Simy Danan calls this a potato "soufflé," but it's really a version of a *marcoude.* Boil 1 pound new potatoes (Yukon Gold or Bintje) in their skin until soft. Drain and peel, then mash. Parboil 1 diced peeled carrot for about 5 minutes. Blanch 1 cup green peas for 2 to 3 minutes. Drain and plunge into cold water, then drain again. Fold the carrots, peas, 3 tablespoons chopped fresh flat-leaf parsley, 1 teaspoon *each* salt and ground turmeric, and 1/2 teaspoon freshly ground black pepper into the mashed potatoes. Fold in 8 beaten eggs. Spoon into an oiled baking dish and bake until golden.

: : : : : :

HARISSA

TUNISIAN HOT PEPPER CONDIMENT

Harissa is a hot pepper sauce that can be made with fresh, roasted, or dried peppers. You may purchase it in paste form in small jars or tubes, but it is easy to make. To serve it as a sauce, thin it with olive oil and a little lemon juice. This recipe was given to me by Baroui Karoui, a visiting Tunisian chef who cooked with me at Square One restaurant during a Mediterranean food conference sponsored by the American Institute of Wine and Food.

Makes about 1 *cup*

4 LARGE RED BELL PEPPERS OR PIMIENTOS, SEEDED,
    DERIBBED, AND CUT INTO PIECES
3 LARGE CLOVES GARLIC, MINCED
1 TABLESPOON GROUND CORIANDER
1 TABLESPOON CARAWAY SEEDS, TOASTED AND GROUND
$1^1/_2$ TO 2 TEASPOONS CAYENNE PEPPER
1 TEASPOON SALT
EXTRA-VIRGIN OLIVE OIL AS NEEDED

In a meat grinder, food processor, or blender, grind or puree the bell peppers or pimientos. Strain, pressing on the solids with the back of a large spoon. You should have about $3/4$ cup puree. Stir in the garlic, spices, and salt. Add oil for spoonability.

Note: You can also make this harissa with roasted red bell peppers and roasted fresh hot red peppers.

ALTERNATE HARISSA

3 DRIED ANCHO CHILI PEPPERS, SOAKED IN HOT WATER
    FOR 1 HOUR
3 GARLIC CLOVES, MINCED
2 TEASPOONS CUMIN SEEDS, TOASTED AND GROUND
1 TEASPOON CARAWAY SEEDS, TOASTED AND GROUND
    (OPTIONAL)
1 TEASPOON SALT
CAYENNE PEPPER TO TASTE
EXTRA-VIRGIN OLIVE OIL FOR FILMING

Drain the peppers. In a blender, combine the peppers, garlic, and seasonings. Puree to a paste. Pack in a hot sterilized jar and film the top with olive oil. Seal and refrigerate for up to 6 weeks.

Note: Harissa, the Tunisian hot sauce, is not to be confused with *harisa,* a very early version of the *d'fina,* which was made with boiled wheat or semolina dough and meat and served on the Sabbath.

: : : : : :

RAS *al* HANOUT *and* HNOT

TWO MOROCCAN-JEWISH SPICE MIXTURES

Most Moroccan Jews prepare their own spice mixtures rather than buying them at a Market. Commercial ras al hanout is often made with the cantharides beetle, for its red color, which makes the mixture not kosher. Ras al hanout is used for meat dishes, onion confit, and so on. Hnot is used in flavoring meatballs and stews.

RAS AL HANOUT:

Combine equal parts by weight cinnamon, cardamom, mace, nutmeg, dried bell peppers *(nioras)* or sweet paprika, black pepper, turmeric, and ground ginger. Toast the spices in a dry pan over low heat until fragrant. Grind in spice mill. Store in a tightly sealed jar.

HNOT:

Combine equal parts by weight cumin, turmeric, mace, nutmeg, cayenne, and dried rose petals and pinches of cinnamon, dried orange peel, and green aniseed (some versions just combine mace, nutmeg, cinnamon, and black pepper). Toast the spices in a dry pan over low heat until fragrant. Grind in spice mill. Store in a tightly sealed jar

: : : : : :

CITRONS CONFITS

PRESERVED LEMONS

While you can use fresh lemons in many North African recipes, preserved lemons add a distinctive note to any dish. Unique in flavor and texture, they are a signature condiment in the North African kitchen. Preserved lemons must be prepared 3 to 4 weeks before using. Keep a constant supply in your pantry and you'll probably find a way to use them even in dishes that are not North African in inspiration. I like them in vinaigrettes and as an addition to many fish recipes and vegetable dishes.

16 LEMONS (ABOUT 4 POUNDS), SCRUBBED
KOSHER SALT AS NEEDED
FRESH LEMON JUICE AS NEEDED

Put the lemons in a nonaluminum container and cover with cold water. (If you have time, soak them for 3 days, changing the water at least once a day. If not, soak for at least a few hours.) Drain the lemons and dry them well. Cut them into lengthwise quarters with a sharp knife but do not cut through the bottom of the lemon. Spoon 1 heaping tablespoonful salt into the center of each lemon. Put 1 heaping tablespoon salt into the bottom of each of 4 hot, sterilized pint jars and add the salted lemons, packing them in tightly. Cover with fresh lemon juice.

Seal the jars. Store in a dry place for 3 to 4 weeks before using, turning the jars upside down and right-side up periodically the first few days. Do not be alarmed if a white film forms on the lemons; it will wash off. Refrigerate after opening. Unopened jars will keep for up to 1 year.

To use the lemons, rinse well under running water. Squeeze the juice from the lemon, remove the pulp, and discard it. Cut the peel into thin slivers or fine dice.

Variation: Alternative Quick Brine Dissolve $1/3$ cup kosher salt in 1 cup boiling water. Put 4 lemons (quartered, as above) in a hot, sterilized pint jar. Pour the brine over them and seal. Store in the pantry for 2 weeks, turning occasionally.

: : : : : :

SAVORY PASTRIES

chapter 2

SAVORY PASTRIES   These are labors of love. To make them, the women of the family and the extended family worked together as a team. Gathered around a table, they drank tea, chatted, and made dozens of these elegant little pastries for special holidays, weddings, or bar mitzvahs. With more and more women working outside the home, these homemade pastries are becoming a memory. And that is too bad, because they are delicious and can be a family signature creation. Called *bestels* (from the Spanish *pastel,* for "pie"), *b'stilla, briouats,* and *briks* in North Africa, and *sambousak,* or *sbanik,* in Syria, Lebanon, and Iraq, they are symbols of hospitality and celebration. Some are stuffed with spiced meat or chicken. Other pastries are filled with an assortment of cheeses, or greens such as spinach or chard enhanced with pine nuts and raisins or tangy olives. The dough can be a short crust, a yeast-raised dough, flaky filo, or a special paper-thin semolina pastry called *ouarka* in Morocco and *malsouka* in Tunisia, or in French, *feuilles de brik,* all translating as "leaves" because they are so thin. Some pastries are baked; some are fried for extra crunch.

Briks are filled with tuna or spiced potatoes and a whole egg, posing a challenge as to how to take a bite and not get egg on your face or your shirt. The most spectacular pie is the *b'stilla,* filled with chicken or squab, sweetened almonds, and a savory egg mixture, served at weddings and other major family celebrations. *Mounas*—orange-scented challah-type breads—might be formed into the initial of your first name when served to break the fast on Yom Kippur, instead of the more conventional braid or round loaf. *Kaak* are sold everywhere as sort of a midday snack or appetizer cracker, like the southern Italian *taralli.*

BESTELS *de la* VIANDE

NORTH AFRICAN MEAT-FILLED PASTRIES

Bestels resemble *borekas:* thin layers of dough wrapped around a savory filling. However, instead of using an oil-based short or flaky pastry, Moroccan *bestels* are traditionally made with *ouarka,* called *malsouka* in Tunisia. *Ouarka* means "leaf" in Arabic, and the French call this pastry *"feuilles* (leaves) *de brik."* The pastry is made with a rather springy semolina dough pressed in an overlapping circular pattern onto a hot pan called a *tobsil* and then peeled off when the paper-thin film of dough has set. Because the process is so time-consuming, most North African cooks buy *ouarka* from those who specialize in making it, rather than attempting to make it at home. *Feuilles de brik* can be purchased from a food wholesale company called Gourmet France, but the minimum order is about 250 sheets. The good news is that you can make bestels with filo dough or egg roll wrappers. Bestels come in two shapes, triangular and rectangular, the latter of which is also called a *cigare* or a *briouat.* These pastries are served during Rosh Hashanah and at special dinners.

As if to corroborate the Spanish roots of *bestels,* both Maguy Kakon, in her book *La cuisine juive du Maroc de mère et fille,* and Viviane Moryoussef, in *Moroccan Jewish Cookery,* call the meat filling *miga,* a Spanish term for bread crumbs enriched with meat juices. Every family seasons the meat mixture in a different way. Simy Danan uses less garlic, but adds a chopped onion. She omits cinnamon but uses ginger and adds 1 teaspoon ground turmeric. Helene Ganz Perez adds the juice of 1 lemon. Leone Jaffin's Algerian *bestel* filling uses 3 large onions to ¹/₂ pound meat, and nutmeg instead of cinnamon or ginger. *Bestels* can be completely assembled and refrigerated until you are ready to cook them.

Makes 2 dozen small pastries

For the filling:

1 POUND GROUND BEEF OR LAMB

1 SMALL ONION, GRATED

2 TO 12 CLOVES GARLIC, CHOPPED

SALT AND FRESHLY GROUND BLACK PEPPER TO TASTE

1 TEASPOON GROUND CINNAMON

¹/₂ TEASPOON GROUND GINGER

1 TEASPOON GROUND TURMERIC (OPTIONAL)

4 TABLESPOONS OLIVE OIL, OR MORE AS NEEDED

2 TABLESPOONS CHOPPED FRESH CORIANDER (CILANTRO)

1 EGG, LIGHTLY BEATEN

JUICE OF 1 LEMON (OPTIONAL)

12 SHEETS *FEUILLES DE BRIK* OR FILO DOUGH, OR
   12 SQUARE EGG ROLL WRAPPERS

1 EGG WHITE, LIGHTLY BEATEN

MELTED MARGARINE OR CANOLA OIL FOR BRUSHING
   AND DEEP-FRYING

To make the filling, in a medium bowl, combine the meat, onion, garlic, spices, and 2 tablespoons of the oil. Mix well. In a large sauté pan or skillet, heat the remaining 2 tablespoons of oil over medium heat. Add the seasoned meat and stir until it starts to lose its red color. Add the fresh coriander and a bit more oil if needed. Cook until the meat browns. Stir in the egg. Add the lemon juice, if using. Remove from heat and let cool.

To assemble the *bestels:* If using *feuilles de brik,* cut the circles in half and place 1 tablespoon filling in center of each. Brush edges with beaten egg white and seal.

If using filo, cut the sheets crosswise into thirds. Brush one strip with margarine or oil and place another strip on top. Brush again, then place 1 scant tablespoon meat filling in the upper corner. Fold up like a flag, into a triangle. Or, to roll them up, place a thin strip of filling along the long side of the filo and fold the ends over by 1 inch. Roll up like a cigar, sealing the edge with egg white. If using egg roll wrappers, roll them up like a cigar, as above.

Cook at once or cover loosely with aluminum foil and refrigerate until you're ready to cook, up to 24 hours.

To fry: In a deep saucepan or a wok, heat 3 inches of oil to 365 degrees F. Fry the pastries in batches until golden, turning once. Using a skimmer, transfer to paper towels to drain.

To bake: Preheat the oven to 400 degrees F. Bake on parchment-lined baking sheets until golden, about 25 minutes.

Variation: Bestels de Fromage (Cheese Filling) Combine $3/4$ pound shredded Gruyère cheese with $1/4$ pound fromage blanc (or cottage or farmer cheese) and 2 eggs lightly beaten. Add a few chopped fresh mint leaves (or 1 small mint leaf per pastry). Another cheese filling adds a mashed potato, 1 teaspoon ground turmeric, and $1/2$ teaspoon ground nutmeg to the cheese mixture, but no mint.

Variation: Bestels des Blettes (Algerian Swiss Chard Filling) Combine 2 pounds Swiss chard leaves or spinach, blanched, drained, and coarsely chopped, with 2 chopped hard-cooked eggs. Season with salt and pepper and add 1 teaspoon ground cumin.

Variation: Bestels à la Pommes de Terre et au Fromage (Algerian Potato and Cheese Filling) Combine 3 large potatoes, boiled in salted water and mashed with 2 tablespoons milk, with $2/3$ cup shredded Gruyère cheese, 2 minced cloves garlic, 2 tablespoons chopped fresh flat-leaf parsley, and 1 egg yolk, and season to taste with salt, pepper, and nutmeg.

Note: Melted butter may be used to assemble meatless bestels.

: : : : : :

B'STILLA

MOROCCAN CHICKEN AND ALMOND PIE

The *bestel* to top all *bestels*, *b'stilla* is a dish of celebration, served at weddings, bar mitzvahs, and other
festive occasions. The origins of this dish are hotly
debated. Was it an Arabic dish brought to Spain, or
a Hispano-Arabic dish brought to Morocco from
Andalusía? Perhaps it was a Spanish dish that emigrated to the Ottoman Empire with the Jews. At
this point, the origin of the dish is speculation, so
it pays to just enjoy it because it is a masterpiece of
Moroccan cuisine. This sweet and savory pie is traditionally made with *ouarka* and fried. Filo sheets are
used here instead, and the oven, as it's easier to bake
the pie than to try to fry it. Although squab is the
deluxe traditional filling, chicken works as well.

Serves 12 TO 14 *as an appetizer,* 6 TO 8 *as a main course*

For the poultry filling:

4 POUNDS SQUAB OR POUSSIN WITH GIBLETS,
   CUT INTO HALVES OR QUARTERS, OR 2 POUNDS
   CHICKEN BREASTS
SALT AND FRESHLY GROUND BLACK PEPPER TO TASTE
$1/4$ CUP VEGETABLE OIL, OR AS NEEDED
1 LARGE ONION, CHOPPED (ABOUT $1^1/2$ CUPS)
$1/4$ CUP CHOPPED FRESH CORIANDER (CILANTRO)
2 TABLESPOONS CHOPPED FRESH FLAT-LEAF PARSLEY
1 TEASPOON GROUND GINGER
1 TEASPOON GROUND CUMIN
$1/2$ TEASPOON CAYENNE PEPPER
$1/2$ TEASPOON GROUND TURMERIC
$1/2$ TEASPOON GROUND CINNAMON
$1/8$ TEASPOON SAFFRON THREADS, CRUSHED
1 CUP WATER

2 TABLESPOONS FRESH LEMON JUICE (OPTIONAL)
8 EGGS, BEATEN

For the almond filling:

3 TO 4 TABLESPOONS VEGETABLE OIL
$1^1/2$ CUPS SLIVERED BLANCHED ALMONDS
2 TABLESPOONS GRANULATED SUGAR
$1/2$ TEASPOON GROUND CINNAMON

8 TABLESPOONS MARGARINE, MELTED
1 POUND FILO DOUGH
3 TABLESPOONS CONFECTIONERS' SUGAR
1 TABLESPOON GROUND CINNAMON
WHOLE BLANCHED ALMONDS FOR GARNISH (OPTIONAL)

To make the poultry filling, sprinkle the birds or
breasts with salt and pepper (reserve the giblets from
the birds). In a large sauté pan or skillet, heat the oil
over medium heat and brown the birds evenly, turning
often. Transfer to a platter. Add the onion and giblets
to the pan and cook over medium heat for about 10
minutes. Add the herbs, spices, and water. Bring to
a boil. Return the birds or breasts to the pan, reduce
heat to low, cover, and simmer for about 30 minutes,
or until the birds or breasts are tender. Remove from
the pan and let cool to the touch. Remove all meat and
skin from the bones and shred into strips, discarding
the skin if you like. You should have about 4 cups
shredded meat. Set aside.

Cook the liquid in the pan over high heat to reduce
to about $1^3/4$ cups. Add the lemon juice, if using.
Reduce heat to low. Stir the eggs into the pan liquids
and cook, stirring constantly, over very low heat until
very soft curds form. Season with salt and pepper.
Drain the cooked egg mixture in a strainer. Set aside.

To make the almond filling, in a large sauté pan or
skillet, heat the oil over low heat and fry the almonds
for about 5 minutes, stirring occasionally, until golden

brown. (Or, to reduce the amount of oil, put the almonds on a baking sheet and bake in preheated 350 degree F oven until golden, about 8 minutes.) Drain on paper towels. Coarsely chop. Toss with the sugar and cinnamon. Set aside.

To assemble, brush a 10- or 12-inch pie plate or a 14-inch pizza pan with the margarine. Add 6 sheets filo, brushing each one with margarine, arranging them like the spokes of a wheel and overlapping them so that the pan is covered and parts of the filo overhang the pan. Be sure to brush the overhanging pieces. Sprinkle half of the almond filling in a 10-inch round area in the center. Spoon half the egg mixture over the almonds. Top this with all of the shredded squab or chicken. Spoon on the rest of the egg mixture, then the rest of the almonds. Fold the overhanging filo over the eggs and almonds. Add 6 to 8 more sheets of margarine-brushed filo on top, then tuck the overhanging pieces under the *b'stilla*. The pie can be refrigerated at this point, loosely covered with aluminum foil.

Preheat the oven to 350 degrees F. Bake the pie until golden on top, about 20 minutes. Drain the excess oil. Flip the pie over onto another pan. Bake for 10 to 15 minutes to brown the bottom. Turn one more time. Bake for 5 minutes. Slide the pie out onto a serving platter or serve from the baking pan. Combine the confectioners' sugar with the cinnamon in a small bowl and stir to blend. Sprinkle the pie with the cinnamon sugar while still warm and run crisscrossing lines over the top. Top with the whole almonds, placed in a decorative pattern, if using. Cut into wedges with a sharp serrated knife and serve warm.

Note: In a pinch, boneless, skinless chicken breasts may be used in place of chicken with bones. They will cook faster.

: : : : : :

BRIKS *à l'OEUF*

TUNISIAN FRIED PASTRIES WITH EGG

The small savory pastry called *bestel* or *briouat* in Morocco is called *brik* in Tunisia. In Algeria, they are called *burak*. *Briks* are made with sheets of *malsouka*, the Tunisian name for *ouarka*, or *feuilles de brik,* and they are deep-fried. To make the *brik,* you can use filo, but egg roll wrappers work like a dream. *Briks* may be filled with cooked meat, poultry, canned tuna, or mashed potatoes, usually with a whole egg nested on top of the filling and the pastry carefully sealed without breaking the egg. The meat version is usually lamb seasoned with onions, cumin, paprika, cayenne pepper, and parsley or cilantro. Other fillings are seasoned mashed potatoes or cooked chicken with cooked potatoes and onions. Egg-filled *briks* must be eaten very carefully if you don't want to drip egg yolk on your shirt.

At an American Institute of Wine and Food dinner I fried one hundred egg-filled *briks,* for Tunisian chef Abderrazak Haouari. In truth, we were not supposed to add the raw eggs because everyone was dressed up, but Haouari insisted that we had to do it the right way. We received no complaints and no dry cleaning bills.

Serves 8

1 TABLESPOON OIL, PLUS MORE FOR DEEP-FRYING

1 ONION, CHOPPED

12 OUNCES CANNED TUNA, DRAINED AND MASHED

2 TABLESPOONS CHOPPED FRESH FLAT-LEAF PARSLEY

1 OR 2 TABLESPOONS FRESH LEMON JUICE

SALT AND FRESHLY GROUND BLACK PEPPER TO TASTE

PINCH OF CAYENNE PEPPER OR HARISSA (PAGE 48)

2 TABLESPOONS CAPERS, RINSED AND CHOPPED

8 SHEETS SQUARE EGG ROLL WRAPPERS OR FILO DOUGH

8 SMALL EGGS

1 EGG WHITE, LIGHTLY BEATEN

In a medium sauté pan or skillet, heat the 1 tablespoon oil over medium heat. Sauté the onion until soft, about 10 minutes. Let cool slightly and mix with the tuna. Add the parsley, lemon juice, salt, pepper, and cayenne or harissa and capers. If using egg roll wrappers, place equal parts of filling on each one, spoon a depression into the filling, and break an egg into each depression. Brush the edges of the wrapper with egg white and fold over to make a 1/2-inch rim. If using filo, brush each sheet with oil, place the filling in the middle, then fold in half, leaving 1 inch on either side. Brush the edges with egg white. Fold in the left side, then the right, then fold up the bottom third to cover.

In a deep saucepan or a wok, heat 3 inches of oil to 365 degrees F. Deep-fry the briks in batches until crisp and golden. Using a slotted spoon or wire skimmer, transfer to paper towels to drain. Serve hot and eat carefully.

Variation: Moroccan Tuna Filling (a recipe from **Fleur de safran)** Combine 12 ounces canned tuna with 1/4 cup chopped fresh flat-leaf parsley, 3 diced boiled potatoes, 2 chopped hard-cooked eggs, 1 minced clove garlic, salt, and pepper to taste, and a pinch of ground mace.

Variation: Potato Filling Boil 2 large and cubed potatoes until soft and mash them. Add 1 finely chopped onion and 3 minced cloves garlic that have been sautéed in 2 tablespoons olive oil until tender. Season with 1 teaspoon salt, 1/2 teaspoon freshly ground black pepper, 1/4 cup chopped fresh flat-leaf parsley, and 2 tablespoons chopped fresh coriander (cilantro). Stir in 1 beaten egg. Capers are an optional addition.

: : : : : :

SAMBUSAKS

ARABIC FILLED PASTRIES

Savory filled pastries are a holiday staple of the Iraqi, Syrian, and Egyptian Jews. These little semicircular turnovers, whose name is of Persian origin, may be filled with cheese or meat. Those filled with cheese can have a butter-based crust, but meat-filled *sambusaks* use margarine or oil in the dough.

Makes about 3 dozen pastries

1/2 CUP (1 STICK) MARGARINE, OR UNSALTED BUTTER FOR
    CHEESE PASTRIES
1/2 CUP OLIVE OIL
1/2 CUP WARM WATER
1 TEASPOON SALT
4 CUPS ALL-PURPOSE FLOUR

For the Syrian cheese filling:
1 POUND FETA CHEESE, MASHED OR CRUMBLED
2 EGGS
1/4 CUP CHOPPED FRESH MINT, OR 2 TABLESPOONS
    DRIED MINT
FRESHLY GROUND WHITE PEPPER TO TASTE

1 EGG, LIGHTLY BEATEN
6 TABLESPOONS SESAME SEEDS
CANOLA OIL FOR DEEP-FRYING (OPTIONAL)

In a small saucepan, melt the margarine or butter over low heat but do not let it bubble. Remove from heat and add the oil, water, and salt. Transfer to a food processor and pulse once to combine. Gradually add the flour, pulsing after each addition. The dough will be very soft and should not stick to the sides of the bowl. On a lightly floured work surface, divide the dough into 8 pieces. Roll out each piece into a thin layer and cut into 3-inch rounds.

To make the filling, in a medium bowl, combine all the ingredients. Stir to blend. Place 1 heaping teaspoon filling on each pastry round and fold in half to make a semicircle. Seal the edges with a fork.

To bake: Preheat the oven to 400 degrees F. Place the pastries on ungreased baking sheets, brush with beaten egg, sprinkle with sesame seeds, and bake until golden, about 20 minutes. Serve at once.

To fry: In a deep saucepan or a wok, heat 3 inches of oil to 365 degrees F. Dip the *sambusaks* in sesame seeds and deep-fry in batches until golden. Using a slotted spoon or wire skimmer, transfer to paper towels to drain. Serve at once.

Variation: Egyptian Meat Filling In a large sauté pan or skillet, heat 2 tablespoons olive oil over medium heat and cook 2 finely chopped onions until tender, about 10 minutes. Add 1 teaspoon ground cinnamon and 1/2 teaspoon ground allspice and cook for 2 minutes longer. Add 1 pound ground lamb and cook, stirring, until it changes color, about 5 minutes. Stir in 1/4 cup pine nuts and season with salt and freshly ground black pepper to taste. Simmer until the meat is juicy but not liquid. Remove from heat and let cool completely.

SAMBUSAK B'TAWAH

IRAQI CHICKEN AND CHICKPEA PASTRIES

While Iraq is not directly on the Mediterranean, these *sambusaks* are so closely related to the Syrian ones I could not leave them out. You may use the dough in the classic *sambusak* recipe (see page 62) or you may use the one listed here.

Makes about 36 sambusaks

For the filling:

16 OUNCES COOKED CHICKPEAS ($^{1}/_{2}$ CUP DRIED)
    (CANNED ARE OK)
$^{1}/_{4}$ CUP OLIVE OIL
2 ONIONS, CHOPPED
1 SMALL GREEN BELL PEPPER, CHOPPED
$^{1}/_{2}$ TEASPOON TURMERIC
2 TEASPOONS GROUND CUMIN
SALT AND FRESHLY GROUND PEPPER TO TASTE
2 CUPS CHOPPED COOKED CHICKEN
2 EGGS, LIGHTLY BEATEN

For the alternate dough:

4 CUPS ALL PURPOSE FLOUR
1 CUP CHICKPEA COOKING LIQUID
1 TEASPOON SALT
$^{1}/_{3}$ CUP OLIVE OR VEGETABLE OIL

CANOLA OIL FOR DEEP-FRYING

Mash the chickpeas coarsely with a fork. Do not make them too smooth. You want some texture. Warm the oil in a sauté pan over medium heat and cook the onions and bell pepper for about 8 minutes. Add the spices and cook 3 minutes longer. Add the chicken and the chickpeas and cook for a few minutes. Then stir in two eggs and cook for a minute or two. Cool the filling.

To make the dough, combine all ingredients in a bowl. Knead until you have a smooth dough. Pinch off a walnut size ball of dough. Roll into 3-inch circle. Place a generous spoonful of filling in the middle. Fold in half. Seal the edges with a fork.

To fry: In a deep saucepan or a wok, heat 3 inches of oil to 365 degrees F. Deep-fry the *sambusaks* in batches until golden. Using a slotted spoon or wire skimmer, transfer to paper towels to drain. Serve at once.

: : : : : :

SBANIK *bil* AJEEN

LEBANESE SPINACH TURNOVERS

Made with a yeast-raised pastry rather than a *sambusak* short crust, these Lebanese spinach pies can be prepared a few hours ahead of time and reheated. A half cup of raisins or pomegranate seeds is occasionally added to the spinach filling. The dough is also used to make *lahm bil ajeen,* the lamb-topped pizza that is popular all over Turkey, Lebanon, and Syria (see below).

Makes 12 pies

For the dough:
1 PACKAGE ACTIVE DRY YEAST
$^3/_4$ CUP LUKEWARM WATER
3 CUPS ALL-PURPOSE FLOUR
1$^1/_2$ TEASPOONS SALT
2 TABLESPOONS OLIVE OIL

1 POUND SPINACH, STEMMED AND COARSELY CHOPPED
   (2 BUNCHES)
SALT TO TASTE
2 TABLESPOONS OLIVE OIL, PLUS MORE FOR BRUSHING
1 CUP CHOPPED ONION OR GREEN ONIONS
1 TEASPOON GROUND ALLSPICE
6 TABLESPOONS PINE NUTS, TOASTED
$^1/_4$ CUP FRESH LEMON JUICE
3 TABLESPOONS CHOPPED FRESH MINT
$^1/_2$ TEASPOON FRESHLY GROUND BLACK PEPPER

To make the dough, stir the yeast into the water and let sit until foamy, about 5 minutes. In a medium bowl, stir the flour and salt together. Stir in the yeast mixture and the oil. On a lightly floured work surface, knead briefly. Shape the dough into a ball. Place in an oiled bowl and turn dough to coat. Cover with a damp towel and let rise in a warm place until doubled, about 1$^1/_2$ hours.

Sprinkle the spinach with salt and place in a colander. Let stand for 1 hour. Squeeze the moisture out of the spinach. Chop it finely.

In large sauté pan or skillet, heat the 2 tablespoons oil and cook the onion until tender, about 5 minutes. Add the allspice and cook 1 minute longer. Stir in the chopped spinach and cook, stirring occasionally, until it wilts. Stir in the pine nuts, lemon juice, mint, and pepper, and more salt if needed.

Preheat the oven to 400 degrees F. Divide the dough into 12 balls. On a lightly floured work surface, roll each piece out into a 6-inch round. Spoon about $^1/_3$ cup spinach mixture into the center of each round. Bring up 3 edges of the round and seal them to make a triangle. You may also form them into half-moons.

Arrange the pastries on a lightly oiled baking sheet and bake until golden, 15 to 20 minutes. Remove from the oven and brush the top of the pastries with oil. Serve warm.

Variation: For a meat filling, use the filling for *sambusaks* (page 62).

Variation: Lahm bil Ajeen (Lamb Flat Bread)
Use the *shanik* dough above and the Egyptian meat filling on page 62, adding $^3/_4$ cup chopped, seeded, and peeled plum tomatoes and 2 tablespoons tamarind puree or fresh lemon juice. Roll the pastry out into 6-inch rounds and spread the lamb mixture on top, leaving a $^1/_2$-inch rim. Bake on lightly greased pans in a preheated 400 degree F. oven until golden brown, about 20 minutes.

: : : : : :

MOUNAS

ALGERIAN ORANGE BREAD

This recipe is a combination of one in Irene and Lucienne Karsenty's book *La cuisine de pied noir* and one from Joelle Roesinger as transcribed by Leone Jaffin in *150 recettes et mille et un souvenirs d'une juive d'Algérie*. Instead of making round loaves, they braid it like challah to serve after the Yom Kippur fast. Gilda Angel's version omits the orange and the seeds and adds ½ cup *each* raisins and toasted almonds to the basic sweet dough. At Yom Kippur, these breads may be baked in the shape of the initials of family members.

Makes 4 small loaves

1 ENVELOPE ACTIVE DRY YEAST

½ CUP SUGAR

½ CUP LUKEWARM WATER

4 CUPS ALL-PURPOSE FLOUR

3 EGGS

2 TABLESPOONS GRATED ORANGE ZEST

2 TABLESPOONS ANISEEDS

2 TABLESPOONS SESAME SEEDS

3 TABLESPOONS UNSALTED BUTTER, MELTED

3 TABLESPOONS PEANUT OIL

2 TEASPOONS SALT

1 EGG YOLK, MIXED WITH 3 TABLESPOONS WATER

2 TABLESPOONS CONFECTIONERS' SUGAR

In a medium bowl, combine the yeast, ¼ cup of the sugar, and the water. Stir in ½ cup of the flour and cover the bowl. Let rest until doubled, about 1 hour, to make a sponge mixture.

In a large bowl, combine the eggs, the remaining ¼ cup sugar, the orange zest, and seeds. Stir lightly. Beat in the melted butter and the oil. Set aside and let rest while the sponge rises.

In a heavy-duty mixer fitted with a paddle, combine the sponge mixture, egg mixture, and 1½ cups of the flour; beat for 3 minutes. Change to the dough hook and add the remaining 2 cups flour and the salt. Knead for 5 minutes. Place the dough in an oiled bowl, turn the dough to coat it, and cover with a damp cloth. Let rise in a warm place until doubled, about 2 hours. Divide the dough into 4 round or cylindrical loaves. Place them on baking sheets lined with lightly floured parchment paper. Cover with a damp towel or plastic wrap and let rise in a warm place until doubled, about 1 hour.

Preheat the oven to 350 degrees F. Slash the top of each loaf in a few places. Glaze the loaves with the egg yolk mixture and dust with confectioners' sugar. Bake until the loaves are golden and sound hollow when tapped on the bottom, 30 to 40 minutes. Let cool on wire racks.

Note: A Moroccan version of this bread uses ¾ cup (1½ sticks) butter, ¾ cup water, and 1 teaspoon of salt, and omits the confectioners' sugar.

: : : : : :

KAAK

SESAME RING PASTRIES

All over the Middle East, street vendors display these savory bread rings on long poles. Called *kaak,* or *semit,* these can be eaten for breakfast or as a snack with cheese. Tunisian Jews make a slightly sweet and salty version of the pastries, which are also called *kaak* but don't use a yeast-based dough.

Makes about 16 *rings*

4 CUPS ALL-PURPOSE FLOUR

1 TEASPOON SALT

^{2}/$_3$ CUP MILK

2 TABLESPOONS UNSALTED BUTTER

1 ENVELOPE ACTIVE DRY YEAST

2 TABLESPOONS SUGAR

^{1}/$_2$ CUP LUKEWARM WATER

1 EGG, BEATEN WITH 2 TABLESPOONS WATER

^{1}/$_2$ CUP SESAME SEEDS

Sift the flour and salt into a large bowl. In a small saucepan, heat the milk over low heat until bubbles form around the edge. Add the butter and let cool to lukewarm.

In a small bowl, combine the yeast, sugar, and water. Stir to dissolve. Let set until foamy, about 5 minutes. Add the yeast mixture to the milk mixture, and gradually stir into the flour mixture. Mix well to make a soft dough that does not stick to the sides of the bowl. Knead with a dough hook until the dough is smooth and elastic, about 8 minutes, or knead by hand for about 15 minutes.

Put the dough in an oiled bowl and turn the dough to coat it. Cover with a damp towel or plastic wrap and let rise in a warm place until doubled, 1^1/$_2$ to 2 hours.

Divide the dough into 16 pieces. With floured hands and on a floured work surface, roll each piece into a long, thin rope. Join the ends of each rope together to make a ring 6 to 7 inches in diameter. Place the rings 2 inches apart on parchment-lined or lightly oiled baking sheets. Brush each ring with the egg mixture, then sprinkle with the sesame seeds. Let rise in a warm place for about 30 minutes.

Preheat the oven to 425 degrees F. Bake for 7 to 10 minutes, then lower the oven temperature to 325 degrees F and continue to bake until the rings are golden brown and sound hollow when tapped, about 20 minutes. Let cool on wire racks.

: : : : : :

VEGETABLES, SALADS, AND GRAINS

AJLOUK *de* POTIRON : : : : : TUNISIAN SQUASH PUREE

HLOU : : : : : SQUASH *and* APRICOT PUREE

AJLOUK *d'*AUBERGINE : : : : : HAOUARI'S SPICY EGGPLANT PUREE

ZAHLOUK, *or* SALADE *d'*AUBERGINES : : : : : EGGPLANT SALAD
au CITRON CONFIT   *with* PRESERVED LEMON

CHOUKCHOUKA, *or* MISHWYIA : : : : : ROASTED PEPPER *and* TOMATO SALAD

SALADE *de* CAROTTES *et* CUMIN : : : : : MOROCCAN CARROT SALAD *with* CUMIN

SLATA FILFIL, *or* FEFLA : : : : : HAOUARI'S ROASTED PEPPER SALAD

SALADE *d'*ORANGES : : : : : MOROCCAN ORANGE SALAD *with* OLIVES

SALADE *d'*ARTICHAUTS CUIT *à l'*ORANGE : : : : : ARTICHOKES COOKED *with* ORANGE

SALADE MERK HZINA : : : : : MOROCCAN CHOPPED SALAD

BAZARGAN : : : : : SYRIAN CRACKED-WHEAT SALAD

ARTICHAUTS, FENOUILS, *et* CÉLERI-RAVES : : : : : ARTICHOKES, FENNEL, *and* CELERY ROOT
au CITRON   *with* LEMON

POIVRONS *de la* VEUVE : : : : : THE WIDOW'S PEPPERS

MUJADDARA : : : : : RICE *and* LENTIL PILAF

ROZ *me* SHAREEYEH : : : : : SYRIAN RICE *with* VERMICELLI

COUSCOUS

RAGOUT *d'*OLIVES VERTS : : : : : POTATO *and* GREEN OLIVE STEW

★

VEGETABLES, SALADS, AND GRAINS

From the length of this chapter it is evident that the Sephardic Jews of the Southern Mediterranean were greatly enamored of vegetables. If not for space concerns, I could have doubled the amount of recipes and still just scratched the surface of their vegetable-dish repertoire. In this chapter, I have combined salads and vegetables because most dishes that are called "salads" are primarily cooked vegetables that have been sliced, chopped, or pureed and usually served at room temperature.

Certain vegetables are associated primarily with the Jews. Eggplant and artichokes were brought to Spain by the Arabs and were adopted by the Jews, who were among the first to try them. They introduced them to Northern Europe as they fled Spain after the Inquisition. Fennel and spinach were also popular. The Jews were actively involved in commerce, so they were among the first to try the vegetables from the New World. Pumpkin, squashes, tomatoes, peppers and chilies, potatoes, and green beans made it onto their table, then were transported throughout the Christian and Muslim worlds. Jews were also known for their love of onions, leeks, and garlic. (Non-Jews even thought that the smell of garlic served to keep disease away from the Jewish community, while others suffered.)

Symbolically, the seven vegetables of Rosh Hashanah reflect the Jews' love and reverence for all vegetables such as spinach, beet greens or chard, leeks, peas or favas, carrots, turnips, pumpkin, and quince, which is a fruit but was one of the revered seven. Vegetables were a major part of the Passover celebration as well, with artichokes, fennel, favas, and peas just coming into season. Grain was also served every day, for economy and nourishment. Rice, couscous, barley, and wheat were often the center of a platter, surrounded by braised vegetables and legumes.

AJLOUK *de* POTIRON

TUNISIAN SQUASH PUREE

Ajlouk is a Tunisian Jewish term for a mashed vegetable side dish. It may be served as part of a *mezze*
assortment at the start of the meal. You can make
this with mashed cooked pumpkin or butternut
squash, or with zucchini. Rather than bake the
squash, some cooks boil it. However, I prefer the
deeper flavor of baked squash. The mixture of caraway, coriander, harissa, and garlic is known as
tabil, a signature spice blend of Tunisian cuisine.

Serves 4 TO 6

1 1/2 POUNDS PUMPKIN OR BUTTERNUT SQUASH

2 TABLESPOONS OLIVE OIL

1 TEASPOON GROUND CARAWAY

1 TEASPOON GROUND CORIANDER

2 CLOVES GARLIC, MINCED

1/2 TEASPOON HARISSA (PAGE 48)

SALT TO TASTE

3 TABLESPOONS FRESH LEMON JUICE

Preheat the oven to 400 degrees F. Cut pumpkin in
half and place face down on a baking sheet; butternut
squash may be baked whole. Bake until soft, about
1 hour. Seed, scoop out the flesh, and mash coarsely.

In a small sauté pan or skillet, heat the oil over low
heat. Add the caraway and coriander and stir until
fragrant. Add the mashed squash, garlic, and harissa
and heat through. Season with salt and lemon juice.
Serve at room temperature, with bread.

Variation: Ajlouk al Q'uara (Zucchini Salad) Use
4 thinly sliced zucchini instead of pumpkin or squash.
Cook in lightly salted boiling water until soft. Drain,
mash, and season as above. Garnish with black olives.

: : : : : :

HLOU

SQUASH AND APRICOT PUREE

Hlou is a Rosh Hashanah specialty served as an
accompaniment to couscous. In the Tunisian version, dried apricots are combined with squash puree
and occasionally dried chestnuts. Some Moroccan
cooks make this sweet puree without the apricots,
using honey for sweetness and omitting the onions.
Kitty Morse, in her book *Come with Me to the
Kasbah,* recalls a similar sweet pumpkin dish that
her family called *cassolita,* a specialty of Tetouan.
(The name is derived from *cazuela,* a Spanish terra-
cotta casserole.) Instead of apricots, she uses raisins
and almonds for the note of sweetness. In Italian-
Jewish cooking, there is a similar dish called *zucca
disfatta,* which uses citron instead of apricots.

Makes about 3 *cups*

1 1/2 CUPS (1/2 POUND) DRIED APRICOTS, CUT INTO
   SMALL PIECES

1/2 CUP SUGAR

1/2 CUP OLIVE OIL

2 ONIONS, FINELY CHOPPED

1 POUND BUTTERNUT SQUASH, PEELED, SEEDED, AND
   CUT INTO 1/2-INCH DICE

2 CUPS WATER

1/4 CUP FRESH LEMON JUICE, OR TO TASTE

1 TEASPOON GROUND CINNAMON

SALT TO TASTE

Soak the apricots in hot water for 1 hour to soften
them. Drain the apricots. In a medium, heavy
saucepan, heat the sugar and oil over high heat until
the sugar is melted and pale caramel in color. (Don't
worry if some sugar solidifies. It will melt as the
onions cook.) Add the onions, reduce heat, and cook,
stirring occasionally, until tender, about 10 minutes.

Add the squash and water and cook until the squash is tender, about 20 minutes. Add the apricots, lemon juice, and cinnamon and cook until you have a slightly chunky puree. Test for salt. Serve warm or at room temperature.

: : : : : :

AJLOUK *d'*AUBERGINE
HAOUARI'S SPICY EGGPLANT PUREE

Over the years it has been my pleasure to cook alongside Tunisian chef Abderrazak Haouari, who lives on the Island of Djerba. Although he is not Jewish, he is well acquainted with Tunisian Jewish food. A unique colony of Jews resided on Djerba, and it is the site of the oldest continually active synagogue in the world. Because of Haouari's friendship with Paula Wolfert, he has been an active participant at many Mediterranean conferences sponsored by the Culinary Institute of America and the American Institute of Wine and Food. I have been happy to act as his sous-chef for many meals and have learned a great deal about Tunisian flavors by tasting food with him. (One time during Ramadan, he fasted while he cooked and I was the person who seasoned and tasted the food.)

Some of the recipes in this chapter are dishes Haouari served at the Mediterranean conference at Hyde Park. Portion sizes vary according to how many dishes you offer as part of the *mezze* assortment. Although he uses 1 head of garlic in this dish, you may want to cut back to 6 cloves. Raw garlic and harissa have quite a kick. Incidentally, the name *ajlouk* refers to Tunisian Jewish mashed-vegetable dishes.

Serves 6

3 GLOBE EGGPLANTS

1 FRESH HOT RED PEPPER

1 SMALL HEAD GARLIC, CLOVES SEPARATED, PEELED, AND CHOPPED, OR FEWER CLOVES TO TASTE

JUICE OF 1 LARGE LEMON

2 TO 3 TABLESPOONS HARISSA (PAGE 48), OR TO TASTE

1 TEASPOON GROUND CARAWAY

7 TABLESPOONS OLIVE OIL

SALT TO TASTE

Preheat the broiler or heat a stovetop griddle over high heat and broil or cook the eggplants and red pepper, turning occasionally, until soft. Or, bake in a preheated 400 degree F oven until soft, turning occasionally. Peel the eggplants, remove the large seed pockets, and mash the pulp. Peel, seed, and finely chop the red pepper. In a medium bowl, combine the eggplant, red pepper, garlic, lemon juice, harissa, and caraway. Stir in the olive oil and season with salt.

: : : : : :

ZAHLOUK, *or* SALADE *d'*AUBERGINES *au* CITRON CONFIT

EGGPLANT SALAD WITH PRESERVED LEMON

Zahlouk, a classic eggplant salad, appears on both the Muslim and the Jewish table in Morocco. This version is from Simy Danan, whose family lived in Fez after emigrating from Andalusía. Some cooks substitute 3 large peeled tomatoes in place of, or in addition to, the roasted peppers, and add a few tablespoons of grated onion. While preserved lemon is a signature ingredient of Fez, chopped lemon pulp or fresh lemon juice may be used instead. If using preserved lemon, add it gradually, as its flavor can be very intense. According to Gilda Angel, this salad or one of its many variations is served to break the fast after Yom Kippur.

Serves 4 TO 6

2¹/₂ TO 3 POUNDS GLOBE EGGPLANTS

¹/₂ CUP PEANUT OR OLIVE OIL, OR AS NEEDED

2 RED BELL PEPPERS, ROASTED, PEELED, AND CHOPPED (PAGE 75)

3 CLOVES GARLIC, MINCED

PEEL OF ¹/₂ PRESERVED LEMON (PAGE 50), MINCED, OR MINCED PULP OF ¹/₂ FRESH LEMON

1 TEASPOON GROUND CUMIN

1 TEASPOON SWEET PAPRIKA

1 TEASPOON SALT

¹/₄ CUP CHOPPED FRESH FLAT-LEAF PARSLEY

Cut alternating strips of peel lengthwise from the eggplant. Cut the eggplant into ¹/₂-inch-thick crosswise slices. In a large sauté pan or skillet, heat the oil over medium heat and fry the eggplant slices until tender, about 8 minutes. Using a slotted spatula, transfer to paper towels to drain. When cool enough to handle, cut the eggplant into 1-inch pieces. In a large bowl, combine with all the remaining ingredients. Mix well and serve at room temperature or cold.

Note: To reduce the amount of oil in this recipe, bake the eggplants or cook them on a cast-iron griddle. To bake, prick each eggplant in a few places with a fork. Place on a baking sheet and roast in a preheated 450 degree F oven until tender but not mushy, turning occasionally, about 45 minutes. Let cool to the touch, then cut into 1¹/₂-inch cubes. Drain in a colander, then transfer to a large bowl. You will need to mix some oil into the salad for flavor and texture.

: : : : : :

CHOUKCHOUKA, *or* MISHWYIA

ROASTED PEPPER AND TOMATO SALAD

Sometimes called *choukchouka,* sometimes *mishwyia,* this classic salad is traditionally served as a starter course but would make a fine accompaniment or sauce with cooked fish or meat. It is a staple in the North African pantry. Simy Danan's Moroccan version is fairly piquant, with spices and lemon. Leone Jaffin's Algerian version is much milder, with no lemon. She serves this salad at Rosh Hashanah and also suggests using it as a filling for an Algerian version of a *coca,* a turnover pastry that is popular in the Balearic Islands off Catalonia. Tunisians might turn this into a quasi-niçoise salad by garnishing it with canned tuna, olives, and hard-cooked eggs.

Serves 8

4 POUNDS RIPE TOMATOES, ROASTED, PEELED, AND CHOPPED

2 POUNDS GREEN BELL PEPPERS, ROASTED, PEELED, AND CHOPPED (PAGE 75)

5 CLOVES GARLIC, MINCED

1 TABLESPOON SALT

1 TABLESPOON SWEET PAPRIKA

1/2 TEASPOON FRESHLY GROUND BLACK PEPPER

6 TABLESPOONS PEANUT OR OLIVE OIL

1 LARGE JÁLAPENO OR HOT RED PEPPER, SEEDED AND
   MINCED (OPTIONAL)

1/2 PRESERVED LEMON (PAGE 50), RINSED AND MINCED,
   OR MINCED PULP OF 1/2 FRESH LEMON (OPTIONAL)

1/2 TEASPOON GROUND CUMIN (OPTIONAL)

3 TO 4 TABLESPOONS CHOPPED FRESH FLAT-LEAF
   PARSLEY OR FRESH CORIANDER (CILANTRO)

In a large sauté pan or skillet, combine all the ingredients except the parsley or fresh coriander. Simmer over medium-low heat until all of the water is evaporated from the tomatoes and the mixture is as thick as a marmalade, about 30 minutes. Serve warm or at room temperature, sprinkled with the parsley or fresh coriander.

Variation: Choukchouka aux Oeufs (Roasted Pepper and Tomato Salad with Eggs) Add eggs to the pan and cook until the whites are set and the yolks are runny. Another version of this recipe (in *La cuisine d'Afrique du Nord*) adds 8 beaten eggs and serves it as an omelet, or *ojja*. Serve warm or at room temperature.

Tunisian Variation: La makbouba is a spicy version of the Algerian *choukchouka*. Tunisian chef Abderrazak Haouari sautés 2 pounds ripe tomatoes, cut into wedges; 1 pound green bell peppers, cut into strips; 1/4 pound sweet red bell peppers, cut into strips; 1/4 pound hot red peppers, chopped; 1/2 pound zucchini, sliced; and 6 to 8 cloves garlic, chopped, in 7 tablespoons olive oil with a few tablespoons of water until tender. Season with salt and lemon juice or cayenne to taste.

: : : : : :

SALADE *de* CAROTTES *et* CUMIN

MOROCCAN CARROT SALAD WITH CUMIN

North African carrot salads can be savory, spicy, or sweet. The carrots may be cut into rounds or julienne, or cooked until soft enough to be mashed. Simy Danan cooks her carrots whole in water with a smashed clove of garlic, then cuts them into 1/2-inch rounds. Helene Ganz Perez, in *Marrakech la rouge*, cuts the carrots into rounds before cooking. An Algerian version of the recipe increases the garlic to 3 cloves, adds a pinch of ground caraway, and uses vinegar instead of lemon. You may prepare cooked beets with the same dressing.

Serves 4 TO 6

1 POUND CARROTS, PEELED

1 CLOVE GARLIC, SMASHED

1/4 CUP FRESH LEMON JUICE

1 TEASPOON GROUND CUMIN

1 TEASPOON SWEET PAPRIKA

1/8 TEASPOON CAYENNE PEPPER (OPTIONAL)

2 TABLESPOONS OLIVE OIL

SALT TO TASTE

Cut the carrots into thin slices or strips. Cook in salted boiling water with the clove of garlic until tender, 5 to 8 minutes. Drain. While warm, toss with the drained garlic, lemon juice, and spices. Stir in the olive oil and season with salt.

Variation: Mzoura (Tunisian Carrot Salad) With their propensity for heat, the Tunisians add a bit of fiery harissa to their carrot salad. Cut the carrots into rounds. Cook in salted boiling water for about 5 minutes, then drain well. In a medium sauté pan or skillet, heat 5 tablespoons olive oil over medium heat and add 5 cloves garlic, minced; 1 or 2 teaspoons harissa mixed with 6 tablespoons water; 1 teaspoon *each* ground caraway and cumin; $1/4$ cup white wine vinegar; and 1 teaspoon salt. Add the carrots and cook until the liquid is mostly absorbed, about 5 minutes. Garnish with chopped fresh flat-leaf parsley or fresh coriander (cilantro) and serve warm or at room temperature.

: : : : : :

SLATA FILFIL, *or* FEFLA
HAOUARI'S ROASTED PEPPER SALAD

Plates of roasted peppers are often on the appetizer table, but leave it to chef Abderrazak Haouari to add the Tunisian heat. Of course, you may make this without the red peppers and with less garlic, but you'd be missing the touch that distinguishes this salad from the pack. As in Italy and France, this pepper salad, sometimes called *fefla,* is garnished with strips of anchovy along with the olives.

Serves 6 TO 8

2 RED BELL PEPPERS

2 YELLOW BELL PEPPERS

2 FRESH HOT RED PEPPERS

1 HEAD GARLIC, CLOVES SEPARATED, PEELED, AND
    MINCED

1 TEASPOON GROUND CARAWAY

1 TEASPOON GROUND FENNEL

SALT AND FRESHLY GROUND BLACK PEPPER TO TASTE

7 TABLESPOONS OLIVE OIL

JUICE OF 1 LEMON

$3^{1}/_{2}$ OUNCES OIL-CURED BLACK OLIVES

THIN STRIPS OF PEEL FROM 1 PRESERVED LEMON
    (PAGE 50)

ANCHOVY STRIPS (OPTIONAL)

Light a fire in a charcoal grill, preheat a gas grill to high, or preheat a broiler. (You may also char the peppers over an open flame on a gas stovetop.) Grill or broil the peppers, turning as needed to char them on all sides. Place in a covered container until cool to the touch, about 20 minutes. Remove the peel by scraping it away with a knife. Remove the seeds and cut the peppers into strips. In a medium bowl, combine the peppers, garlic, and spices. Add the oil and lemon juice. Toss to mix. Decorate with olives, strips of preserved lemon, and anchovies, if using.

Note: Some versions of this salad add chopped tomatoes.

: : : : : :

SALADE *d'*ORANGES

MOROCCAN ORANGE SALAD WITH OLIVES

Refreshing, colorful, and a perfect foil for spicy foods, orange salads are popular throughout Morocco. The oranges can be peeled and cut into rounds or into segments. They may be paired with thinly sliced radishes for a subtle hint of heat. Sometimes, they are dressed with sugar and lemon juice and a sprinkling of either cinnamon or hot pepper. This version comes from Jacqueline Cohen-Azuelos's *Fleur de safran*.

Serves 6 TO 8

2 POUNDS BLOOD ORANGES AND 1 POUND BITTER
   ORANGES OR BERGAMOTS, OR 3 POUNDS ORANGES,
   PEELED AND CUT INTO SEGMENTS OR ROUNDS
1 TEASPOON GROUND CUMIN
1 TEASPOON SWEET PAPRIKA
1 TEASPOON GROUND CINNAMON
2 CLOVES GARLIC, MINCED (OPTIONAL)
SALT AND FRESHLY GROUND BLACK PEPPER TO TASTE
JUICE OF 2 LEMONS
1/4 CUP OLIVE OIL
2 CUPS (1/2 POUND) BLACK OLIVES, PITTED
1 BUNCH FRESH CORIANDER (CILANTRO), STEMMED

Put the orange segments or rounds in a terra-cotta dish or ceramic bowl. Sprinkle with the spices, garlic, salt, and pepper. Toss with the lemon juice and olive oil. Top with the black olives and toss again. Let rest for 30 minutes, then toss again. All of the flavors should mingle and penetrate the oranges. Decorate with leaves of fresh coriander at serving time.

: : : : : :

SALADE *d'*ARTICHAUTS CUIT *à l'*ORANGE

ARTICHOKES COOKED WITH ORANGE

I just love Yolande Rouas's Algerian artichoke and orange salad. Cooking artichokes with tangy slices of citrus fruit provides a bright contrast to their slightly bitter flesh. Orange segments may be added for a colorful garnish, but the tartness of lemon is essential for flavor balance.

Serves 6

JUICE OF 1 LEMON
6 LARGE ARTICHOKES
2 TABLESPOONS PEANUT OIL
3 CLOVES GARLIC, MINCED
PINCH OF CRUSHED SAFFRON THREADS
1 ORANGE, PEELED AND THINLY SLICED
1 LEMON, PEELED AND THINLY SLICED
1/4 CUP WATER
SALT AND FRESHLY GROUND BLACK PEPPER TO TASTE

Fill a large bowl with water and add the lemon juice. Trim the artichokes by cutting off the stems flush with the bottom. Remove all the leaves from the artichokes, scoop out the chokes, and place the artichoke hearts in the lemon water until ready to cook.

In a large saucepan, heat the oil over low heat. Drain the artichoke hearts and add them to the pan with the garlic, saffron, orange and lemon slices, and water. Season with salt and pepper. Cover and cook until the artichokes are tender, 15 to 25 minutes. Check the water level to see that the artichokes don't scorch, although if they caramelize a bit they are very tasty. Serve warm or at room temperature.

Note: You can also cut the hearts into 1/3-inch-thick slices and cook them for 12 to 15 minutes.

: : : : : :

SALADE *d'*ORANGES ★ MOROCCAN ORANGE SALAD WITH OLIVES

SALADE MERK HZINA

MOROCCAN CHOPPED SALAD

Ideal for hot weather, *merk hzina* is the North African version of chopped salad. Maguy Kakon adds a minced small hot red pepper to the mixture. This salad is best dressed ahead of time. Just be aware that the tomatoes give off liquid as the salad sits, so you may need to adjust the seasoning. In Tunisia, a similar chopped salad is called *slata jida* and contains tomatoes, cucumbers, peppers, green onions, lemon, and oil.

Serves 6

6 LARGE RIPE TOMATOES, PEELED, SEEDED, AND DICED

1 RED ONION, FINELY CHOPPED

3 STALKS CELERY, DICED

1 BELL PEPPER, DICED

1 SMALL PRESERVED LEMON (PAGE 50), DICED

2 TABLESPOONS CAPERS

3 TABLESPOONS OLIVE OIL

$1/2$ TEASPOON *EACH* SALT AND FRESHLY GROUND BLACK PEPPER

2 TABLESPOONS CHOPPED FRESH FLAT-LEAF PARSLEY OR FRESH CORIANDER (CILANTRO)

In a salad bowl, combine all of the ingredients except the parsley or fresh coriander. Let sit at room temperature for 2 hours before serving so that the flavors mingle. Sprinkle with parsley or fresh coriander.

: : : : : :

BAZARGAN

SYRIAN CRACKED-WHEAT SALAD

Bazargan is a Syrian Jewish version of tabbouleh. Its name means "of the bazaar." Some versions add chopped hazelnuts or pine nuts to the mix. Though traditionally made with tamarind paste, pomegranate molasses may be substituted.

Serves 6 TO 8

2 CUPS BULGUR WHEAT OR FINELY CRACKED WHEAT

SALT TO TASTE

6 TABLESPOONS OLIVE OIL

2 TABLESPOONS TAMARIND PASTE DISSOLVED IN $1/4$ CUP BOILING WATER, OR 2 TABLESPOONS POMEGRANATE MOLASSES

2 TABLESPOONS TOMATO PASTE

3 TABLESPOONS FRESH LEMON JUICE, OR TO TASTE

2 TEASPOONS GROUND CUMIN

1 TEASPOON GROUND CORIANDER

$1/2$ TEASPOON GROUND ALLSPICE

$1/4$ TEASPOON CAYENNE PEPPER, OR TO TASTE

1 CUP WALNUTS, COARSELY CHOPPED

$1/4$ CUP PINE NUTS, TOASTED (OPTIONAL)

2 TABLESPOONS CHOPPED FRESH FLAT-LEAF PARSLEY

Put the wheat in a bowl and cover with lightly salted water. Let soak until the grains are tender, 30 minutes or longer. Drain well. Transfer to a bowl.

In a small bowl, whisk the olive oil, tamarind mixture, tomato paste, lemon juice, and spices together. Add to the wheat and toss. Season to taste. Fold in the nuts and parsley and mix well. Let sit at room temperature for 4 hours or as long as overnight. Serve at room temperature.

: : : : : :

ARTICHAUTS, FENOUILS, *et* CÉLERI-RAVES *au* CITRON

ARTICHOKES, FENNEL, AND CELERY ROOT WITH LEMON

Leone Jaffin's family in Algeria served this spring vegetable stew at Passover. The artichoke and fennel combination is served as a salad in Tunisia, minus the celery root and with less garlic, but with the addition of, yes, harissa.

Serves 6 TO 8

3 LEMONS

6 ARTICHOKES

1 HEAD GARLIC, CLOVES SEPARATED, PEELED, AND MINCED, OR FEWER CLOVES TO TASTE

$1/4$ CUP CHOPPED FRESH FLAT-LEAF PARSLEY

6 TABLESPOONS PEANUT OIL

2 BULBS FENNEL, TRIMMED AND CUT INTO $1/2$-INCH-THICK SLICES

1 CELERY ROOT, PEELED AND CUT INTO 1-INCH CUBES

$1/4$ CUP WATER

SALT AND FRESHLY GROUND PEPPER TO TASTE

Fill a large bowl with water and add the juice of 1 lemon. Trim the artichokes by cutting off the stems flush with the bottoms. Remove all the leaves from the artichokes, scoop out the chokes, and place the artichoke hearts in the lemon water until ready to cook. Cut one of the lemons into 6 to 8 pieces, and juice the remaining lemon.

In a small bowl, combine the garlic and parsley. In a large saucepan, heat the oil over medium heat. Drain the artichoke hearts and add to the pan, hollow-side up. Fill the hollows with the garlic mixture. Arrange the fennel slices and celery root cubes around the artichoke hearts. Top with the lemon pieces, lemon juice, and water. Sprinkle with salt and pepper. Cover and simmer until the vegetables are tender and caramelized but not scorched, about 45 minutes. Check the liquid level from time to time, adding a bit of water if necessary. Serve warm.

: : : : : :

POIVRONS *de la* VEUVE ★ THE WIDOW'S PEPPERS

POIVRONS *de la* VEUVE

THE WIDOW'S PEPPERS

A signature dish of the Sephardic Jews, stuffed vegetables are usually filled with meat, meat and rice, or just a savory rice mixture, but this recipe uses a bread filling. Daisy Taieb, in *Les fêtes juives à Tunis,* and Andrée Zana-Murat, in *La cuisine juive tunisienne,* both recall this recipe, named for a legendary widow who was too poor to use meat but made a great dish with frugal ingredients.

Serves 8

8 GREEN BELL PEPPERS

4 CLOVES GARLIC

2 CUPS FRESH BREAD CRUMBS, SOAKED IN WATER AND
   SQUEEZED DRY

3 TABLESPOONS CHOPPED FRESH FLAT-LEAF PARSLEY

$1/4$ CUP CHOPPED FRESH CORIANDER (CILANTRO)

1 TEASPOON GROUND CARAWAY

1 TEASPOON GROUND CORIANDER

1 TOMATO, PEELED, SEEDED, AND CHOPPED

2 HARD-COOKED EGGS, DICED

2 EGGS, LIGHTLY BEATEN

SALT AND FRESHLY GROUND PEPPER TO TASTE

Preheat the oven to 350 degrees F. Carefully cut across the top of each pepper and reserve the cap, or "little hat." Scoop out the seeds with a sharp knife. Boil the shells for 5 minutes in lightly salted water. Drain well. In a bowl, combine all the rest of the ingredients to make a filling.

Stuff the filling into the peppers. Place the peppers in a baking pan and add 1 inch of water. Cover the pan and bake until peppers are tender, 25 to 30 minutes.

: : : : : :

MUJADDARA

RICE AND LENTIL PILAF

The lentils for this pilaf must be perfectly cooked: not too soft and not too crunchy. Green or black lentils are best, as they will hold their shape. Brown and red lentils soften quickly and are often too tricky to control. Red onions seem to caramelize more easily, but you can also use yellow or white ones. Most versions of this recipe stir in the onions; I like to stir in half and leave half on top.

Serves 6

1 CUP GREEN OR BLACK LENTILS

5 TABLESPOONS OLIVE OIL

3 LARGE RED ONIONS, SLICED

SALT AND FRESHLY GROUND BLACK PEPPER TO TASTE

$1/4$ TEASPOON GROUND CINNAMON

1 CUP BASMATI RICE

2 TABLESPOONS CHOPPED FRESH FLAT-LEAF PARSLEY
   (OPTIONAL)

Rinse and pick over the lentils. In a medium saucepan, combine the lentils and salted water to cover. Bring to a boil, reduce heat to a simmer, cover, and cook until tender but firm, 25 to 30 minutes, but keep watching! You don't want to overcook these.

In a large sauté pan or skillet, heat the oil and sauté the onions, stirring often, until deep golden brown, about 20 minutes. Stir in the salt, pepper, and cinnamon. Drain on paper towels.

Cook the rice until al dente, about 20 minutes. Add to the lentils and toss to combine. Stir in half the onions. Taste and adjust the seasoning. Top with the remaining onions. Serve warm or at room temperature, garnished with parsley, if using.

Variation: Kitchree Omit the onions and add 1 cup tomato sauce, 1 tablespoon minced garlic, and 1 teaspoon ground cumin to the rice and lentil mixture.

Variation: Imjadra (Bulgur Pilaf with Lentils) Substitute bulgur wheat for the rice.

Note: In Egypt, the combination of lentils and rice may be called *koshari* and is served with a spicy tomato sauce or a green chili and garlic salsa. Occasionally, fideos or vermicelli are added to the mixture.

: : : : : :

ROZ *me* SHAREEYEH

SYRIAN RICE WITH VERMICELLI

Rice and noodles are a popular side dish in most of the Arab countries. If serving this at a meat meal, use oil and water or meat or poultry broth. If served at a dairy meal, you may use butter and water or vegetable broth.

Serves 4 TO 6

1½ CUPS BASMATI RICE
2 TABLESPOONS UNSALTED BUTTER OR OLIVE OIL
½ CUP BROKEN FIDEOS OR VERMICELLI NOODLES
   (1-INCH PIECES)
3 CUPS WATER OR BROTH
1 TEASPOON SALT

Rinse and drain the rice in a fine-mesh sieve.

In a medium saucepan, melt the butter or heat the oil over medium heat and sauté the noodles, stirring often, until golden brown. Stir in the rice until all the grains are coated. Add the water or broth and salt. Bring to a boil and cook until the water has been partly absorbed and little holes appear in the top of the rice. Cover, reduce heat to a simmer, and cook until the rice is tender, about 20 minutes.

: : : : : :

COUSCOUS

Couscous is made with semolina flour and water. The dough is rolled into pellets that are then pushed through screens to create smaller pellets of a uniform size. Traditionally, couscous is steamed atop a stew in a *couscoussier*. The top part is called the *keskas*, the bottom part the *tenjra*. Most of us don't have this piece of equipment as part of our *batterie de cuisine*, but we can improvise. Large double boilers with slotted upper compartments will work, and most colanders will fit over a large pot. Even a pasta pot with a basket insert can work; line the basket or colander with cheesecloth. Cheesecloth is necessary only if the holes are large; the steam rising from below keeps the couscous aloft in the *couscoussier*. (Couscous that doesn't swell sufficiently when cooked may continue to swell in your tummy. Steaming it over boiling water helps reduce the risk of potential stomach churning.)

The master recipe here is the North African steaming method. The quick and easy variation that follows may be scorned by purists, but it works, is fast, and produces couscous that will puff up enough to prevent stomachache. Holding it over boiling water for a while after cooking will help it to puff more.

Makes 9 TO 10 cups

3 CUPS COUSCOUS

3 TABLESPOONS OLIVE OIL

5 TO 7 CUPS HOT WATER, LIGHTLY SALTED

Put the couscous in a deep baking dish. Rub the couscous with the oil and pour 5 cups of hot water over it. Cover the dish and let the couscous absorb the water. Rake the couscous with your hands or 2 forks to break up the lumps. Transfer it to a colander or steamer basket lined with cheesecloth. Steam over boiling water in a covered pot or steamer for 15 to 20 minutes. Turn the couscous out into a large baking dish and rake it again to break up lumps. Sprinkle with 1 or 2 more cups of hot water, rake it with your fingers, and scoop it back into the colander. Steam again as above for 20 minutes. Transfer to a platter to serve. Leftover couscous can be reheated over boiling water.

QUICK COUSCOUS

3 CUPS COUSCOUS

$4^1/2$ TO $4^3/4$ CUPS BOILING WATER

1 TEASPOON SALT

1 TABLESPOON OIL

Ignore the box instructions that tell you to pour couscous into boiling water. It will cook but it will not be light and may not absorb all of the water evenly. It needs room to expand and swell. Instead, pour the couscous into a baking dish or lasagna pan. Season the boiling water with the salt and oil and pour $4^1/2$ cups over the couscous, stirring well to moisten every piece. Cover the container with plastic wrap. Let rest for 10 to 15 minutes. Rake with a fork to break up lumps. Serve now, or sprinkle the couscous with another $^1/4$ cup hot water and steam it over boiling water in a covered pot for 15 to 20 minutes for additional swelling. If you have been overly exuberant with the water and the couscous seems too wet, let it sit in a warm place and it will gradually absorb all of the water. I promise.

: : : : :

RAGOUT *d'*OLIVES VERTS

POTATO AND GREEN OLIVE STEW

Leone Jaffin's Aunt Olga made this dish quite often for the family. It uses the marinated olives on page 38, which are also a fine staple to have on hand for hors d'oeuvres.

Serves 6

3 TABLESPOONS PEANUT OIL
1 LARGE ONION, FINELY CHOPPED
2¹/₂ POUNDS NEW POTATOES, PEELED AND SLICED
1 TEASPOON SWEET PAPRIKA
1 BAY LEAF
PINCH CAYENNE PEPPER (OPTIONAL)
1 TEASPOON FRESHLY GROUND BLACK PEPPER
2 CUPS (¹/₂ POUND) ALGERIAN SPICED GREEN OLIVES
    (PAGE 38)

In a large sauté pan or skillet, heat the oil over medium heat and sauté the onion for about 5 minutes. Add the sliced potatoes, paprika, bay leaf, and cayenne, if using. Sprinkle generously with pepper, but don't add any salt as the olives are salty enough. Cover the potatoes halfway with water and bring to a boil. Reduce heat to a simmer, cover, and cook for 15 minutes. Add the olives and cook until the potatoes are tender, about 10 minutes.

Variation: If you are as enamored of tiny new potatoes as I am, and also like the idea of round potatoes with round olives, parboil very small whole new potatoes until partially cooked. Sauté the onion and add the spices, olives, whole potatoes, and a bit of water, then cover the pan and cook over medium heat until the potatoes are tender, about 10 minutes.

: : : : : :

SOUPS

chapter 4

✦

SOUPS

Most of these soups are meals in a bowl. Along with bread and a salad or two, they can make a substantial lunch or supper. The soups profit from being made ahead of time and then reheated after the flavors have mellowed and come together. They can be made with water or broth, and they can be legume-and-vegetable based or enriched with meat. Lemon juice and beaten eggs may be added just before serving.

SOUPE *de* COURGE ROUGE
et POIS CHICHES *à la* CORIANDRE

PUMPKIN SQUASH AND CHICKPEA SOUP WITH FRESH CORIANDER

In Moroccan and Tunisian Jewish kitchens, there are numerous versions of this hearty classic, a bean and pumpkin soup. Some cooks use dried favas or white beans instead of chickpeas. Some omit the greens altogether, and some add meat (see *Sopa de Siete Verduras,* page 94). This is a stick-to-your-ribs dish and can be a full meal when paired with bread or a salad.

Serves 6 TO 8

2 CUPS DRIED CHICKPEAS, SOAKED OVERNIGHT AND
    DRAINED

1 LARGE ONION, CHOPPED

1 CARROT, CHOPPED

2 POUNDS BUTTERNUT SQUASH OR PUMPKIN, PEELED
    AND CUT INTO 1-INCH CUBES

8 CUPS CHICKEN BROTH

$1/4$ CUP CHOPPED FRESH CORIANDER (CILANTRO)

SALT AND FRESHLY GROUND PEPPER TO TASTE

$1/2$ TEASPOON GROUND CINNAMON

SUGAR TO TASTE (OPTIONAL)

LEAVES FROM 1 OR 2 BUNCHES SWISS CHARD, CUT INTO
    STRIPS (RESERVE STEMS FOR ANOTHER DISH)

In a soup pot, combine the chickpeas, onion, carrot, and squash or pumpkin. Add the broth and half of the fresh coriander. Bring to boil, reduce heat, cover, and simmer until the chickpeas are tender, about 40 minutes. Pass through a food mill.

Reheat the soup and season with salt, pepper, cinnamon, and sugar, if using. Rinse the chard thoroughly, drain, and put in a large saucepan with the rinse water clinging to it. Place over medium heat and cook until wilted, about 3 minutes. Drain well. Add to the soup and heat through, stirring often to prevent scorching, thinning with water as needed. Sprinkle with the remaining coriander. Serve hot.

: : : : : :

VELOUTÉ VERT *de* PESSAH
GREEN PUREE FOR PASSOVER

I found this beautiful soup in *Fleur de safran: images et saveurs du Maroc* by Jacqueline Cohen-Azuelos. Its lovely green color doesn't fade in the cooking process because half of the fresh coriander is pureed uncooked. For a richer soup, use chicken broth instead of water. You may make this soup without the heart and gizzard garnish, but it is a lovely touch and provides an interesting textural contrast.

Serves 6

5 POUNDS FAVA BEANS, SHELLED

2 1/2 POUNDS GREEN PEAS, SHELLED (ABOUT 2 1/2 CUPS)

1 CARROT, CHOPPED

1 ONION, CHOPPED

2 STALKS CELERY, CHOPPED

1 BUNCH FRESH CORIANDER (CILANTRO) INCLUDING
   SOME STEMS, CHOPPED

4 CUPS WATER OR CHICKEN BROTH

SALT AND FRESHLY GROUND BLACK PEPPER TO TASTE

2 TABLESPOONS PEANUT OR OLIVE OIL

1/2 POUND POULTRY HEARTS AND GIZZARDS, CUT INTO
   BITE-SIZED PIECES

1 CUP CHICKEN BROTH FOR GIZZARDS

Blanch the fava beans in boiling water for 2 minutes. Rinse in cold water and pinch the beans from their skins. In a soup pot, combine the favas, peas, carrot, onion, celery, and half the fresh coriander. Add the water or broth. Bring to boil, reduce heat to a simmer, and cook, skimming if necessary, until the vegetables are tender, about 30 minutes. Add the salt and pepper. Puree the soup with the remaining fresh coriander and set aside.

In a medium sauté pan or skillet, heat the oil over medium-high heat and cook the hearts and gizzards until golden. Add the 1 cup chicken broth and stir to scrape up the browned bits from the bottom of the pan. Cover and simmer until the hearts and gizzards are tender, 30 to 40 minutes.

To serve, add 2 or 3 pieces of hearts and gizzards to each bowl and ladle the hot soup over them.

: : : : : :

BESSARA, *or* BICHRA

FAVA OR LENTIL SOUP

In the Moroccan cities of Fez and Meknes, fava or lentil soup is served during Passover and also at times of mourning. Both favas and lentils are used to make *bessara*. In Tunisia, *bissara*, or *bichra*, has double the garlic, an equal amount of potatoes cooked with the beans, and a bit of harissa. Occasionally some tomato puree is added, but meat is not used as garnish. In Egypt, the juice of 2 lemons is added to the soup. *Bessara* is also the name for a puree of beans served as a dip with pita bread.

Serves 6

1 POUND DRIED FAVA BEANS

2 LARGE CLOVES GARLIC, HALVED

SALT TO TASTE

$^1/_2$ TEASPOON FRESHLY GROUND BLACK PEPPER

1 TO 2 TEASPOONS GROUND CUMIN, OR TO TASTE

1 TABLESPOON SWEET PAPRIKA

$^1/_2$ TEASPOON GROUND TURMERIC (OPTIONAL)

3 OR 4 PIECES *KHLII* (AIR-DRIED MEAT) (OPTIONAL)

1 BUNCH FRESH CORIANDER (CILANTRO), STEMMED AND
   CHOPPED

Rinse and pick over the fava beans. Soak the beans in cold water for 2 to 3 hours. Drain and remove the skins. In a soup pot, combine the favas, garlic, and water to cover. Bring to a boil, reduce heat to a simmer, cover, and cook until tender, about 1 hour. Season with salt, pepper, cumin, paprika, and turmeric, if using. Add the *khlii,* if using, and fresh coriander. Ladle into bowls and serve hot.

Moroccan Variations: The beans may be cooked with a piece of fatty meat instead of adding *khlii* afterwards. Some cooks add spicy beef sausages instead of *khlii*. This soup can also be made with lentils or split peas.

Tunisian Variation: Add spicy *merguez* sausage and the hand-rolled noodles called *hlalem*. Sometimes, chopped Swiss chard is added.

Syrian Variation: Shouraba al adass is lentil soup with the addition of greens and a generous squirt of lemon juice. It may be made with lamb broth and is seasoned with cinnamon and cumin, and enriched with rice or noodles. Sometimes a stalk or two of rhubarb or a few tablespoons of pomegranate syrup are used instead of lemon.

: : : : : :

SOPA *de* SIETE VERDURAS

ROSH HASHANAH SEVEN-VEGETABLE SOUP

In her book *Marrakech la rouge: les juifs de la medina,* Helen Ganz Perez reminisces about the *soupe aux sept legumes* that was part of her family's Rosh Hashanah tradition. The seven "vegetables" are onion, pumpkin, vegetable marrow, zucchini, Swiss chard, chickpeas, and quince. I could not get over how closely it resembles the Andalusían *olla gitana,* or gypsy stew, which uses pears instead of quince. I suspect that the "gypsy" title was added as a cover, after the Jews had left Spain and the recipe remained in the culinary pipeline. Today in Spain, they add ham to flavor the stock, but in pre-Inquisition days the soup was most likely made with beef. You may add diced cooked brisket for a more filling soup (see the variation). In the city of Tetouan, Moroccan cooks add greens and use white beans instead of chickpeas. For a meatless version, use vegetable broth.

Serves 6 TO 8

2/3 CUP DRIED CHICKPEAS, SOAKED OVERNIGHT AND
     DRAINED
3 ONIONS, CHOPPED
8 CUPS BEEF OR VEGETABLE BROTH
2 POUNDS PUMPKIN OR BUTTERNUT SQUASH, PEELED,
     SEEDED, AND DICED
3 ZUCCHINI, CUT INTO ROUNDS
1 SMALL VEGETABLE MARROW, SLICED CROSSWISE, OR
     1 TURNIP OR RUTABAGA, QUARTERED
LEAVES FROM 1 BUNCH SWISS CHARD, CUT INTO STRIPS
     (RESERVE STEMS FOR ANOTHER USE)
2 APPLES, QUINCE, OR PEARS, PEELED, CORED, AND
     DICED
SALT TO TASTE

1/2 TEASPOON GROUND CINNAMON, OR TO TASTE
1 TEASPOON FRESHLY GROUND BLACK PEPPER, OR
     TO TASTE
1 TEASPOON GROUND CUMIN (OPTIONAL)
SUGAR TO TASTE (OPTIONAL)

In a soup pot, combine the chickpeas, onions, and broth. Bring to a boil, reduce heat, and cook covered until almost tender, 45 to 60 minutes. Add the rest of the vegetables and the fruit and simmer until tender, 25 to 30 minutes. Add the salt, cinnamon, pepper, and cumin and sugar, if using. Ladle into bowls and serve hot.

Meat Variation: Gilda Angel refers to a *sopa de la siete verduras y carne,* in which 3 to 4 pounds of brisket or beef shank are cooked with the soaked chickpeas (or dried favas), 2 chopped onions, 1 piece of diced pumpkin, 1/2 teaspoon ground cinnamon, 1 tablespoon sugar, 1 teaspoon pepper, and 8 cups water for 3 hours. Remove the meat and set aside. Puree the soup and add cinnamon, and cumin and sugar, if using. Cut the meat into dice and return it to the soup. Reheat gently and serve hot. I prefer to add the vegetables later so that they hold their shape, and I add the diced meat to the broth after the vegetables are tender.

: : : : : :

SORDA

PASSOVER MATZOH SOUP

Called *sodra* (meaning deaf) by the Turks, *sorda* is the Moroccan version of the classic Passover matzoh soup served in Casablanca and Safi. Why deaf? Maybe because after the matzoh plump up in the soup, they no longer make any crunching sounds. Some cooks add diced tomatoes and chopped fresh coriander to the mix. This version comes from Fortunée Hazan-Arama's *Saveurs de mon enfance*.

Serves 6 TO 8

1^1/$_2$ POUNDS FAVA BEANS, SHELLED

1^1/$_2$ POUNDS BONELESS BEEF, LAMB, OR CHICKEN, CUT INTO BITE-SIZED PIECES

8 CUPS CHICKEN OR MEAT BROTH

^{1}/$_4$ CUP OLIVE OR CANOLA OIL

SALT AND FRESHLY GROUND BLACK PEPPER TO TASTE

^{1}/$_4$ TEASPOON SAFFRON THREADS, CRUSHED

1^1/$_2$ POUNDS GREEN PEAS, SHELLED (ABOUT 1^1/$_2$ CUPS)

3 TO 4 MATZOH

Blanch the fava beans in boiling water for 2 minutes. Rinse in cold water and pinch off the skins.

In a soup pot, combine the meat, broth, oil, salt, pepper, and saffron. Cover and simmer until half-cooked, 30 minutes for beef and lamb or 15 minutes for chicken. Add the peas and favas. Cover and cook until the meat or chicken is tender, about 1 hour for beef and lamb or 25 minutes for chicken. Break up the matzoh and put the pieces in a soup tureen or individual bowls. Pour the hot soup over.

Tunisian Variation: Soupe au Pain Azyme comes from *la cuisine juive d'Afrique du Nord:* Cut ^{1}/$_2$ pound stewing beef into small pieces and sauté in ^{1}/$_4$ cup oil for 5 minutes. Add 1 chopped onion, 1 teaspoon harissa, and 2 teaspoons sweet paprika; cook for a few minutes. Add 3 sliced leeks, 3 chopped tomatoes, 1 chopped potato, 1 chopped stalk celery, 3 sliced carrots, and water to cover. Simmer for 2 hours, or until tender. Ten minutes before serving, add ^{1}/$_2$ pound broken matzoh, ^{1}/$_4$ cup chopped fresh mint, and ^{1}/$_4$ cup chopped fresh coriander (cilantro).

: : : : : :

H'RIRA *de* KIPPOUR

LEMONY BEAN AND RICE SOUP FOR YOM KIPPUR

H'rira, also called *h'riba* or *harira,* is the classic Moroccan soup served by Muslims and Jews alike to break a fast, whether it be Ramadan or Yom Kippur. It is nourishing and quite filling, a meal in a bowl. The variables are the amount of lentils or chickpeas, rice or pasta, and the choice of meat: beef, lamb, or chicken. This Judeo-Arabic soup is thickened at the end with flour and made tart with lemon juice. A similar soup is called *chorba* in Tunisia.

Serves 8

½ POUND BEEF SHANK MEAT OR LAMB STEWING MEAT
    (SHOULDER), CUT INTO ½-INCH PIECES

1 BAY LEAF

1½ CUPS LENTILS

1 CUP DRIED CHICKPEAS OR DRIED FAVA BEANS, SOAKED
    OVERNIGHT AND DRAINED (REMOVE FAVA SKINS)

2 ONIONS, CHOPPED

2 STALKS CELERY, CHOPPED

4 TOMATOES, PEELED, SEEDED, AND CHOPPED

1 TEASPOON GROUND CINNAMON

½ TEASPOON GROUND TURMERIC

½ TEASPOON GROUND GINGER

1 BUNCH FRESH CORIANDER (CILANTRO), STEMMED AND
    CHOPPED, ABOUT ¼ CUP

½ CUP RICE, ORZO, PASTINA, OR A HANDFUL OF BROKEN
    SPAGHETTI

¼ TEASPOON SAFFRON THREADS, CRUSHED AND
    STEEPED IN 2 TABLESPOONS HOT WATER

2 TABLESPOONS FLOUR, MIXED WITH ¼ CUP WATER

SALT AND FRESHLY GROUND BLACK PEPPER TO TASTE

JUICE OF 1 OR 2 LEMONS, OR TO TASTE

¼ CUP CHOPPED FRESH FLAT-LEAF PARSLEY

Put the meat and bay leaf in a soup pot and add lightly salted water to cover. Bring to a boil, skim, reduce heat, and simmer, covered, until the meat is tender, about 1 hour. Using a slotted spoon, set the meat aside and discard the bay leaf.

Add the lentils, chickpeas or fava beans, onions, celery, tomatoes, spices, and half the fresh coriander to the broth in the pot. Cover and simmer for at least 30 minutes. Return the meat and simmer until the beans are tender. Taste and adjust the seasoning. Add the rice or pasta and the saffron mixture, and cook for 15 minutes. Add the flour mixture and cook over low heat until slightly thickened. Stir in the salt, pepper, lemon juice, parsley, and the remaining fresh coriander. Ladle into bowls and serve hot.

Alternate Method: Put the chickpeas or favas in a large saucepan, add water to cover, and bring to a boil. Reduce heat and simmer, covered, until tender, about 1 hour. Set aside and salt lightly. In a large pot, bring 3 cups water to a boil. Add the lentils and rice, reduce heat and simmer for 20 minutes.

Brown the meat in oil over high heat in a large sauté pan or skillet. Add the onions and spices and fry for 10 minutes. Add water to cover, and the bay leaf and simmer for 30 minutes.

Add the meat and onion mixture to the lentils and rice. Add the chickpeas or favas, tomatoes, parsley, and fresh coriander. Simmer for 15 minutes. Season to taste. The soup should be peppery. Stir in the flour mixture and cook over low heat until slightly thickened. Remove from heat and add the lemon juice.

: : : : :

TFAIA

CHICKEN SOUP WITH EGGS

This egg-enriched chicken soup, similar to Greek *avgolemono,* is served the night before Yom Kippur. The noodles called *inetria* may be added, or rice. During Passover, broken matzoh is stirred in.

Serves 6

1 LARGE STEWING CHICKEN OR 2 BROILERS, CUT INTO
   PIECES (ABOUT 5 POUNDS CHICKEN PARTS)
1 LEMON, HALVED, PLUS 6 TABLESPOONS FRESH
   LEMON JUICE
KOSHER SALT TO TASTE
3 ONIONS, CHOPPED
3 CARROTS, CHOPPED
3 TURNIPS, CHOPPED
1 STALK CELERY, CHOPPED
2 LEEKS (WHITE PARTS ONLY), CLEANED AND CHOPPED
1 TEASPOON SAFFRON THREADS, CRUSHED
BOUQUET GARNI: 3 SPRIGS FRESH FLAT-LEAF PARSLEY,
   2 BAY LEAVES, AND 3 CLOVES, TIED IN A CHEESE-
   CLOTH SQUARE
FRESHLY GROUND BLACK PEPPER TO TASTE
3 PINCHES GROUND CINNAMON
6 EGGS
MINCED FRESH MINT (OPTIONAL)

Remove any excess fat from the chicken pieces, then rinse. Rub each piece with lemon halves and sprinkle with salt. Cover and refrigerate, overnight if possible.

Put the chicken in a large stockpot and add cold water to cover. Bring to a boil. Reduce heat to a simmer and skim the scum from the broth. Simmer gently for 30 minutes. Add the vegetables, saffron, and bouquet garni. Cook for about 2 hours longer. Using a skimmer, remove the solids and discard.

Pour the broth through a sieve lined with wet cheese-cloth into a large bowl. Chill the stock, uncovered, in an ice bath in the sink until cold. Spoon off the fat. Pour the broth into a pot, bring to a boil, and cook at a low boil, skimming if needed, until reduced and flavorful. Add the pepper and cinnamon.

Beat the eggs with the lemon juice and stir into the soup. Simmer for 8 to 10 minutes. Garnish the soup with the mint, if using. Cooked noodles or broken matzoh may be added as well.

: : : : : :

SFAXIA, *or* SOUPE *de* POISSONS

TUNISIAN FISH SOUP FROM SFAX

Andrée Zana-Murat's recipe from *De mère et fille la cuisine juive tunisienne* provided the inspiration for this recipe. Traditionally, large pieces of fish are cooked in the fish broth but served as a separate course. It may be accompanied with sautéed red pimientos, 1 per person, and croutons. A Libyan version uses less fish, cut in smaller pieces, and serves it in the soup but omits croutons.

Serves 6

3 TO 4 POUNDS FIRM WHITE FISH, SUCH AS COD OR
   BASS, CUT INTO STEAKS OR THICK SLICES
SALT AND FRESHLY GROUND PEPPER TO TASTE
JUICE OF $1/2$ LEMON
2 POUNDS FISH HEADS AND BONES
6 TABLESPOONS OLIVE OIL, PLUS MORE FOR FRYING
   CROUTONS
1 LARGE ONION, COARSELY GRATED
8 CLOVES GARLIC, MINCED
1 TABLESPOON SWEET PAPRIKA
1 TABLESPOON TOMATO PASTE
$1/4$ CUP TOMATO PUREE
$1/2$ RED BELL PEPPER, SEEDED, DERIBBED, AND DICED
1 SMALL BULB FENNEL, TRIMMED AND DICED
2 PINCHES SAFFRON THREADS, CRUSHED
1 TEASPOON GROUND CUMIN (OPTIONAL)
$1/2$ BUNCH FRESH FLAT-LEAF PARSLEY, TIED TOGETHER
6 SLICES COUNTRY BREAD, CUT INTO 1-INCH CUBES

Rub the fish with salt, pepper, and lemon juice. Set aside on a plate in the refrigerator. Put the fish heads and bones in a stockpot and add water to cover. Bring to boil, skim, and reduce heat to a simmer. Cover and cook for 30 minutes, then strain. Reserve the stock.

In a large saucepan, heat the 6 tablespoons oil over medium heat and sauté the onion and garlic for about 3 minutes. Remove from heat and add the paprika, tomato paste, and tomato puree and stir well. Return to heat and add the bell pepper, fennel, saffron, and cumin, if using. Add the reserved fish stock and the parsley and simmer for 20 minutes. Add the fish pieces and simmer covered until opaque throughout, 10 to 15 minutes. Do not overcook. Using a slotted spoon, remove the fish pieces and set aside. Remove the parsley and discard.

Film a large sauté pan or skillet with olive oil and heat over medium heat. Add the bread cubes and fry until golden. Drain on paper towels. Serve the broth in bowls with the fish pieces and croutons alongside.

Variation: Caldero Oranais (Algerian Fish Soup)
In Algeria, they serve a fish soup called *caldero,* which is related to the Portuguese *caldeirada* but similar in cooking technique to a classic French *soupe au poisson.* Pieces of fish are cooked in a pureed fish broth lightly scented with tomato and dried sweet peppers (*nioras*). A spoonful of saffron rice is added to each bowl, then some cooked fish and a ladleful of hot soup is spooned on top. The soup is garnished with a spicy harissa-tinged sauce similar to a French *rouille.*

: : : : : :

FISH

chapter 5

FISH

Fish is considered prestigious in the Sephardic kitchen. It is served on Friday night and at the closing Sabbath meal. Thursday-night suppers are often meatless, so fish is also a centerpiece at the table then. For Rosh Hashanah, fish is served with the head on to commemorate the head of the year. The Mediterranean offers abundant varieties of fish, and the recipes for fish are even more abundant. Fish is baked, fried, braised, grilled, and poached. It is topped with tomato sauce or paired with lemon and olives, bathed in spice marinades, or rubbed with spices. It can be stuffed with almonds and bread crumbs and baked. Fish is braised and served with couscous, cut into thick steaks, or ground and rolled into savory fish balls. It may be paired with potatoes. During Passover, crumbled matzoh replaces couscous as an accompaniment. Fish may be served hot or at room temperature, coated in a sesame sauce, or marinated escabeche-style in cumin and lemon. What follows are recipes for some of the best fish dishes I have ever eaten. Even non-fish-lovers will be seduced.

TAGINE KEFTA *mn* HOOT, *or* BOULETTES *de* POISSON

TUNISIAN FISH BALL TAGINE

In Spain, Sephardic fish balls, called *albondigas,* were seasoned simply with parsley and maybe a little cheese, then fried and served with tomato sauce. Tunisian Jewish fish balls are more highly seasoned. To hold the fish together, most cooks use fresh bread crumbs, but Simy Danan uses only dry crumbs and some cooked rice. During Passover, matzoh meal is used. The fish balls may be fried or poached, then simmered in fish broth flavored with tomato puree, and served with couscous. Some recipes use chopped tomatoes and peppers in the broth.

Serves 6 TO 8

For the fish balls:

1¹/₂ POUNDS MILD WHITE FISH, SUCH AS COD, SOLE, SNAPPER, OR BASS

2 TABLESPOONS CHOPPED FRESH FLAT-LEAF PARSLEY

2 TABLESPOONS CHOPPED FRESH CORIANDER (CILANTRO)

3 CLOVES GARLIC, MINCED

2 ONIONS, FINELY CHOPPED

1¹/₂ TEASPOONS KOSHER SALT

¹/₂ TEASPOON HARISSA (PAGE 48)

2 TEASPOONS GROUND CUMIN

4 SLICES STALE BREAD, CRUSTS REMOVED, SOAKED IN WATER AND SQUEEZED DRY, OR 1¹/₂ CUPS FRESH BREAD CRUMBS

1 EGG, BEATEN

OLIVE OIL FOR FRYING

For the tomato sauce:

3 TABLESPOONS OLIVE OIL

2 CLOVES GARLIC, MINCED

6 TABLESPOONS TOMATO PUREE, OR 4 TOMATOES, CHOPPED

2 CUPS FISH BROTH OR WATER

SALT AND FRESHLY GROUND BLACK PEPPER TO TASTE

COUSCOUS FOR SERVING

CHOPPED FRESH FLAT-LEAF PARSLEY FOR GARNISH

To make the fish balls, bone and finely chop the fish. In a food processor or large bowl, combine the fish with all the remaining ingredients except the egg and oil. Mix well. Add the egg and mix until smooth. Dipping a spoon and your fingers in cold water, remove a sample of fish paste and roll into a ball. Fry in a little olive oil and taste and adjust the seasoning. Form the rest of the fish paste into 1-inch balls. Either fry now, or place on a baking sheet lined with parchment paper and refrigerate for up to 3 hours.

In a large sauté pan or skillet, heat ¹/₂ inch oil over medium-high heat and fry a few fish balls at a time until lightly browned. Using a slotted spoon, transfer to paper towels to drain.

To make the tomato sauce, in a large saucepan, heat the oil over medium heat. Add all the remaining ingredients and bring to a boil. Reduce heat to a simmer. Add the fish balls and simmer for 15 minutes. Serve over couscous, sprinkled with parsley.

Variation: Instead of frying the fish balls, Helene Ganz Perez, in her book *Marrakech la rouge,* steams them atop a bed of tomatoes. The fish balls are seasoned with parsley, cinnamon, salt, and pepper, but have no bread filler. To cook them her way, sauté 3 pounds peeled, seeded, and chopped tomatoes in 3 tablespoons peanut oil, sprinkle them with salt, and simmer for 15 minutes. Drain off the excess liquid, as you want the mixture to be fairly thick. Place the fish balls on top of the tomatoes, cover the pan, and simmer for 20 minutes.

Note: This dish can be made more elaborate by adding cooked vegetables such as fennel, peppers, carrots, turnips, zucchini, and/or pumpkin.

: : : : : :

PASTEL *de* MERLAN

WHITING AND POTATO PIE

Not every dish in the Maghrebi kitchen is highly spiced. This fish *pastel* recipe appears in *La cuisine juive d'Afrique du Nord* and in *Moroccan Jewish Cookery* by Viviane and Nina Moryoussef. Layers of mashed potatoes enclose a delicately seasoned chopped fish filling. A tender white fish in the cod family will do in place of the classic whiting. Although the potatoes are boiled, you could bake them if you like. This is an ideal dish for entertaining, as it can be assembled hours ahead of time and refrigerated until you need to bake it. It is also a fine main course during Passover.

Serves 6 TO 8

2 1/2 POUNDS MILD-FLAVORED FISH FILLETS,
    SUCH AS SOLE, CHOPPED OR GROUND
1 BUNCH FRESH FLAT-LEAF PARSLEY, STEMMED AND
    CHOPPED
SALT AND FRESHLY GROUND BLACK PEPPER TO TASTE
1/2 TEASPOON SAFFRON THREADS, CRUSHED
1/2 TEASPOON GROUND MACE
1/2 TEASPOON FRESHLY GRATED NUTMEG
5 EGGS

4 POUNDS RED POTATOES, PEELED AND CUT INTO
    SMALL PIECES, OR 6 TO 8 RUSSET POTATOES
2 TABLESPOONS PLUS 1/2 CUP OLIVE OIL
2 HARD-COOKED EGGS, SLICED
1 EGG YOLK, BEATEN

In a large bowl, mix the fish and parsley together. In a medium sauté pan or skillet, combine the spices with 1/4 inch of water over low heat. Add the fish and mix well with a wooden spoon to make a smooth, dry paste. Let cool. Stir in 2 of the eggs, lightly beaten.

If using red potatoes, cook them in salted boiling water until tender, 15 to 20 minutes. Drain well and stir over low heat until dry. Or, if using russets, bake them in a preheated 400 degree F oven until tender when pierced with a knife, about 1 hour; let cool and peel. Mash the potatoes and mix in 2 tablespoons of the olive oil and the remaining 3 eggs, lightly beaten.

Preheat the oven to 350 degrees F. Oil a large casserole. Spread half the mashed potatoes on the bottom. Cover this with the fish paste, then the sliced hard-cooked eggs. Top with the remaining potatoes. Brush the top with the beaten egg yolk. Pour the 1/2 cup olive oil over the top. Bake until golden, about 45 minutes.

Note: You might want to serve this with a simple tomato sauce or a mild *chermoula* (page 108).

: : : : : :

SAMAK *al* KAMOUN,
or HUT B'CAMOUN

BROILED FISH WITH CUMIN

Cumin is a very popular seasoning for fish in Lebanon, Syria, Egypt, and North Africa. The fish is marinated in a cumin-based spice mélange and grilled or broiled, or it is baked with sautéed onions seasoned with cumin. Just be sure to cut slits in both sides of the fish so that the marinade can penetrate and the fish will cook more evenly. If you don't have a whole fish, you may use fillets.

Serves 6

ONE 3$\frac{1}{2}$- TO 4-POUND WHOLE FISH, SUCH AS STRIPED
    BASS, SNAPPER, OR ROCK COD
3 TEASPOONS KOSHER SALT
6 TABLESPOONS FRESH LEMON JUICE
3 TABLESPOONS CUMIN SEEDS, TOASTED AND GROUND
2 TABLESPOONS SWEET PAPRIKA
2 TEASPOONS MINCED GARLIC
$\frac{1}{2}$ TEASPOON FRESHLY GROUND BLACK PEPPER
$\frac{1}{2}$ CUP OLIVE OIL
$\frac{1}{2}$ CUP CHOPPED FRESH FLAT-LEAF PARSLEY OR FRESH
    CORIANDER (CILANTRO)

Preheat the oven to 450 degrees F. Rub the fish with 2 teaspoons of the salt inside and out, then rinse. Cut diagonal slits in both sides of the fish so the marinade can penetrate.

In a small bowl, combine the lemon juice, spices, garlic, pepper, and the remaining 1 teaspoon salt. Whisk in the olive oil. Rub this paste into the fish, and if baking, wrap in aluminum foil, and bake until opaque throughout, 25 to 30 minutes. Unwrap and serve sprinkled with parsley or fresh coriander. If broiling or grilling there is no need to use foil.

Fillet Variations: Use six 6-ounce mild-flavored white fish fillets, rub with spices, and bake in a pre-heated 450 degree F oven for 8 to 10 minutes, or broil for 4 minutes per side.

: : : : : :

POISSON *aux* POIS CHICHES

FISH WITH CHICKPEAS

Fish with chickpeas is very popular in Morocco, especially in the cities of Fez and Rabat. It is often served during the Rosh Hashanah holidays and on meatless Thursdays or the Sabbath. I have found a few versions of this dish prepared with the richer and oilier shad or sardines, but these may be difficult to find at our markets. A firm fish, such as sea bass, snapper, halibut, or cod, will work very well. Mackerel, if you can find it, is ideal. This dish is particularly delicious served with braised Swiss chard or braised mixed greens.

Serves 4

1 CUP DRIED CHICKPEAS, SOAKED OVERNIGHT AND
   DRAINED
8 CLOVES GARLIC, HALVED LENGTHWISE
1 SMALL HOT RED PEPPER, CHOPPED
1 TEASPOON GROUND TURMERIC
1 TABLESPOON SWEET PAPRIKA
$^1/_2$ CUP CHOPPED FRESH CORIANDER (CILANTRO)
4 TABLESPOONS OLIVE OIL
2 TEASPOONS KOSHER SALT, PLUS MORE FOR
   SPRINKLING
$1^1/_2$ POUNDS FISH FILLETS
1 OR 2 RED BELL PEPPERS, SEEDED, DERIBBED,
   AND DICED
FRESHLY GROUND BLACK PEPPER TO TASTE

In a soup pot, combine the chickpeas, garlic, red pepper, spices, most of the fresh coriander, and 2 tablespoons of the oil. Bring to a boil, reduce heat to a simmer, cover, and cook until the chickpeas are tender, about 1 hour. Add the 2 teaspoons salt and set aside.

Sprinkle the fish with salt. Cover and refrigerate for 1 hour.

In a large sauté pan or skillet, heat the remaining 2 tablespoons oil over medium heat. Sauté the bell peppers until softened.

Pour the chickpeas and their cooking liquid into a large sauté pan or skillet. Arrange the fish fillets over the chickpeas. Add the bell peppers. Bring to a boil, then reduce heat to a simmer, cover, and cook until the fish is opaque throughout, 15 to 20 minutes. Taste the pan juices, and adjust the seasoning. Add the pepper. Sprinkle with the remaining fresh coriander. Serve hot or at room temperature.

: : : : : :

SARDINES MARINÉES
au CITRON *et* CUMIN

SARDINES MARINATED WITH LEMON AND CUMIN

Simy Danan's recipe for marinated sardines is really a classic Spanish *escabeche* with Moroccan spices. The fish can be arranged atop a bed of roasted red and green bell peppers for a colorful (and tasty) presentation.

Serves 4 TO 6

2 POUNDS FRESH SARDINES

10 TO 11 TABLESPOONS OLIVE OIL

2 TABLESPOONS CHOPPED FRESH CORIANDER (CILANTRO)

1 TABLESPOON KOSHER SALT, PLUS MORE TO TASTE

1 TEASPOON FRESHLY GROUND BLACK PEPPER, PLUS
   MORE TO TASTE

2 TABLESPOONS SWEET PAPRIKA

FLOUR FOR DREDGING

JUICE OF 3 LEMONS

1 TABLESPOON GROUND CUMIN

1/2 CUP CHOPPED FRESH FLAT-LEAF PARSLEY

Cut the heads off the sardines, cut them open along the belly, and remove the innards. Remove the bones by pressing along the backbone to open each fish like a book, then snapping off the bone just at the tail. Rinse and dry the fish.

In a shallow platter, combine 2 to 3 tablespoons of the oil with the fresh coriander, the 1 tablespoon salt, the 1 teaspoon pepper, and 1 tablespoon of the paprika. Coat the fish with this mixture.

In a large sauté pan or skillet, heat 4 tablespoons of the oil over medium-high heat. Dredge the fish in flour to coat both sides and fry in batches until golden, turning once. Drain on paper towels and transfer to a serving platter.

In a small bowl, whisk together the remaining olive oil, the lemon juice, the remaining 1 tablespoon paprika, the cumin, and salt and pepper. Pour over the fish and sprinkle with the chopped parsley.

Marinate for 1 to 2 hours. Serve at room temperature.

: : : : : :

POISSON CHERMOULA

FISH KEBABS, OR BROILED FISH WITH CHERMOULA

Chermoula is the classic Moroccan marinade for fish. Whether you plan to bake, grill, fry, or steam fish, marinating it in *chermoula* will only improve its flavor. There are many versions of *chermoula*. For this recipe, choose one of the three offered below.

Serves 6 TO 8

Chermoula No. 1 (from Vivianne and Nina Moryoussef):
1 ONION, FINELY CHOPPED OR GRATED
6 CLOVES GARLIC, MINCED
2 TEASPOONS GROUND CUMIN
1 TEASPOON SWEET PAPRIKA
$1/2$ TEASPOON SAFFRON THREADS, CRUSHED AND MIXED
    WITH 2 TABLESPOONS HOT WATER
$1/2$ CUP CHOPPED FRESH FLAT-LEAF PARSLEY
$1/2$ CUP CHOPPED FRESH CORIANDER (CILANTRO)
6 TABLESPOONS OLIVE OIL
6 TABLESPOONS FRESH LEMON JUICE
KOSHER SALT AND FRESHLY GROUND BLACK PEPPER
    TO TASTE

Chermoula No. 2:
3 CLOVES GARLIC, MINCED
PEEL OF $1/2$ TO 1 PRESERVED LEMON (PAGE 50), RINSED
    AND FINELY MINCED
$1/2$ CUP CHOPPED FRESH CORIANDER (CILANTRO)
$1/2$ CUP FRESH FLAT-LEAF PARSLEY
$1/2$ TEASPOON CAYENNE PEPPER
$1/2$ TEASPOON SAFFRON THREADS, CRUSHED AND
    STEEPED IN 2 TABLESPOONS HOT WATER
1 TEASPOON SWEET PAPRIKA
9 TABLESPOONS OLIVE OIL
$1/4$ CUP FRESH LEMON JUICE

Chermoula No. 3:
2 CLOVES GARLIC, MINCED
$1/2$ CUP CHOPPED FRESH FLAT-LEAF PARSLEY
$1/2$ CUP FRESH CORIANDER (CILANTRO)
1 TEASPOON FRESHLY GROUND BLACK PEPPER
$1/2$ TEASPOON GROUND CINNAMON
$1/2$ TEASPOON GROUND GINGER
$1/2$ TEASPOON SAFFRON THREADS, CRUSHED AND
    STEEPED IN $1/4$ CUP WATER
2 TEASPOONS GROUND CUMIN
1 TEASPOON SWEET PAPRIKA
$1 1/2$ TEASPOONS KOSHER SALT
6 TABLESPOONS OLIVE OIL

2 POUNDS FISH FILLETS (ANY FIRM WHITE FISH
    OR TUNA)
COUSCOUS (PAGE 83) OR COOKED POTATOES FOR SERV-
    ING

To make the *chermoula,* in a mixing bowl, combine all the ingredients and mix to blend. Leave the fillets whole or cut into $1 1/2$-inch cubes for kebabs. Arrange the fillets or kebabs in the baking dish, spoon most of the *chermoula* over them, and marinate in the refrigerator for 2 hours. Preheat the broiler and broil the fish about 4 minutes on each side, then spoon the reserved *chermoula* over the fish after cooking. Or, bake the fish in a preheated 450 degree F oven until opaque throughout, allowing 8 to 10 minutes for each inch of thickness. Drizzle the reserved *chermoula* on top. Serve with couscous or boiled potatoes.

: : : : : :

COUSCOUS DJERBIEN *au* POISSON

FISH COUSCOUS FROM DJERBA

In Tunisia, fish couscous can be a simple affair or an elaborate presentation. Chickpeas are usually added, along with assorted vegetables. In Djerba, five vegetables are used: onions, garlic, tomatoes or tomato paste, green bell peppers, and chickpeas. For Rosh Hashanah you could do this with the classic seven vegetables: onions, tomatoes, sweet potatoes or pumpkin, chickpeas, carrots, turnips, zucchini or greens. In some versions, the sauce is pureed and the plate decorated with strips of green bell pepper and chopped mint or basil. Other versions serve the fish on a platter and pass the couscous and vegetables with the broth separately. This recipe is based on one I cooked with chef Abderrazak Haouari at a special dinner in Los Angeles. One of his signature dishes, it received raves and clean plates, the highest compliment of all.

Serves 8

SALT TO TASTE

2 TO 3 POUNDS MIXED FISH, CUT INTO THICK PIECES
   OR STEAKS

1/4 CUP OLIVE OIL

2 ONIONS, CHOPPED

2 STALKS CELERY, CHOPPED

6 CLOVES GARLIC, MINCED

4 TOMATOES, PEELED, SEEDED, AND CHOPPED

1/2 TEASPOON CAYENNE PEPPER

1 TEASPOON SWEET PAPRIKA

1 TABLESPOON GROUND CUMIN

1/2 TEASPOON FRESHLY GROUND BLACK PEPPER

6 CUPS WATER OR FISH STOCK

1 CUP COOKED CHICKPEAS

3 CARROTS, PEELED AND CUT INTO 1-INCH ROUNDS
   (OPTIONAL)

2 TURNIPS, PEELED AND CUT INTO 2-INCH PIECES
   (OPTIONAL)

8 TO 12 SMALL NEW POTATOES, HALVED (OPTIONAL)

FRESH LEMON JUICE TO TASTE (OPTIONAL)

3 OR 4 TABLESPOONS CHOPPED FRESH MINT (OPTIONAL)

COUSCOUS COOKED WITH WATER OR PART FISH BROTH,
   SEASONED WITH A LITTLE OLIVE OIL OR BUTTER
   (PAGE 83)

1 TABLESPOON HARISSA (PAGE 48)

Lightly salt the fish, cover, and refrigerate. In a large, heavy saucepan or soup pot, heat the oil over medium heat. Add the onions, celery, and garlic and cook for 8 minutes. Stir in the tomatoes and spices. Cook for about 2 minutes, then add the water or stock, chickpeas, and carrots and turnips, if using. Simmer for 15 minutes. Add the fish and potatoes, if using, and simmer until the potatoes are tender and the fish opaque throughout, 15 to 20 minutes. Add lemon juice or some chopped mint, if using.

To serve, put a generous spoonful of couscous into each of 8 individual soup bowls. Ladle the fish and vegetables around, then spoon on some of the broth. Or, pile the couscous on a large platter, make a well in the center, and put the fish in the middle and place the vegetables around. Ladle some broth over the top and serve the rest separately. Pass the harissa, thinned with some of the broth.

Note: During Passover, serve the fish stew and broth with crumbled matzoh.

: : : : : :

POISSON FARCI *aux* AMANDES

BAKED FISH STUFFED WITH ALMOND PASTE

In traditional Moroccan kitchens, a very sweet almond paste filling is stuffed inside a whole fish, which is then baked. In this version, however, the filling is savory and is a combination of two recipes, one from *Moroccan Jewish Cookery,* by Viviane and Nina Moryoussef, who attribute it to the town of Essaouira, and one from *La cuisine juive d'Afrique du Nord,* by Jeanne Ifergan.

Serves 6

ONE 4-POUND WHOLE FISH, SUCH AS SEA BASS,
    SNAPPER, OR SALMON

2 TO 3 TABLESPOONS KOSHER SALT, PLUS MORE
    TO TASTE

1$^1/_2$ CUPS BLANCHED ALMONDS, TOASTED AND CHOPPED

1 CUP FRESH TOASTED BREAD CRUMBS

$^1/_2$ TEASPOON GROUND MACE

$^1/_2$ TEASPOON FRESHLY GRATED NUTMEG

3 HARD-COOKED EGGS

3 EGGS

FRESHLY GROUND BLACK PEPPER TO TASTE

$^1/_4$ CUP CHOPPED FRESH FLAT-LEAF PARSLEY

For the sauce:

6 TABLESPOONS OLIVE OIL

1 ONION, FINELY CHOPPED

6 CLOVES GARLIC, MINCED

$^1/_2$ TEASPOON SAFFRON THREADS, CRUSHED AND
    STEEPED IN $^1/_4$ CUP WATER

1 TEASPOON KOSHER SALT

$^1/_2$ TEASPOON FRESHLY GROUND BLACK PEPPER

2 TOMATOES, SLICED

1 LEMON, PEELED AND ALL PITH REMOVED, SLICED
    PAPER THIN

Rub the fish with the 2 or 3 tablespoons kosher salt inside and out and rinse well.

In a food processor, combine the almonds, bread crumbs, spices, and hard-cooked eggs. Pulse briefly to mix. Add the raw eggs, salt and pepper, and parsley. Pulse quickly to combine. Pack this mixture into the fish and skewer it closed. Put the fish in an oiled baking pan or dish.

To make the sauce, preheat the oven to 400 degrees F. In a small sauté pan or skillet, heat 2 tablespoons of the olive oil over medium heat and cook the onion for about 10 minutes. Add the garlic, saffron infusion, salt, and pepper. Cook 2 minutes longer. Spoon the onion mixture over the fish. Arrange the sliced tomatoes and lemon over the fish and drizzle with the remaining oil. Bake until fish is opaque throughout, about 30 minutes. Serve warm or at room temperature.

: : : : : :

POISSON SAUCE SOLEIL

FISH WITH GOLDEN SAUCE

The turmeric and saffron in this sauce create the illusion of fish bathed in golden sunlight. This dish is often served in Morocco during the Rosh Hashanah holiday. A variation on this recipe adds 2 cups green olives at the end of cooking. Serve with parsleyed new potatoes.

Serves 4

2 SMALL LEMONS, PEELED AND CUT INTO THIN ROUNDS

1 TABLESPOON GROUND TURMERIC

SALT TO TASTE

OLIVE OIL FOR DRIZZLING, PLUS 1 TABLESPOON

4 CLOVES GARLIC, MINCED

$1/2$ TEASPOON SAFFRON THREADS, CRUSHED AND
    STEEPED IN $1/4$ CUP WARM WATER

1 BUNCH FRESH CORIANDER (CILANTRO), STEMMED AND
    CHOPPED

FOUR 6-OUNCE FISH STEAKS OR FILLETS, SUCH AS
    SWORDFISH, HALIBUT, SEA BASS, OR COD

FRESHLY GROUND BLACK PEPPER TO TASTE

1 CUP ($1/4$ POUND) PITTED GREEN OLIVES (OPTIONAL)

GROUND CUMIN FOR SPRINKLING

Put the lemon slices in a shallow bowl or on a platter and sprinkle with the turmeric and salt. Press down on the lemon slices with a fork to extract some juice. Drizzle with a bit of olive oil and set aside.

In a large sauté pan or skillet, heat the 1 tablespoon olive oil over medium heat and sauté the garlic for 2 to 3 minutes; do not let it color. Stir in the saffron infusion. Arrange the lemon slices on the bottom of the pan, reserving all of the accumulated juices. Sprinkle with half the chopped fresh coriander.

Arrange the fish fillets on top. Sprinkle with salt and pepper, the reserved lemon juice, the remaining fresh coriander, and the olives, if using.

Bring to a boil, reduce heat to low, cover, and simmer until opaque throughout, about 10 minutes. Sprinkle with cumin. Serve hot or warm.

Note: You may also layer the fish and lemon in a baking dish and bake in a preheated 450 degree F oven for 8 to 10 minutes.

: : : : : :

SARDINES MARIÉES

MARRIED SARDINES

These "married" sardines are joined together with a love potion of spiced potatoes.

Serves 4 TO 6

4 POUNDS FRESH SARDINES

For the filling:

1 POUND BINTJE OR YUKON GOLD POTATOES, PEELED
    AND CUT INTO CHUNKS

3 TABLESPOONS CHOPPED FRESH FLAT-LEAF PARSLEY

3 TABLESPOONS CHOPPED FRESH CORIANDER (CILANTRO)

3 CLOVES GARLIC, MINCED

3 EGGS

1 TEASPOON GROUND CUMIN

1 TABLESPOON SWEET PAPRIKA

$1/2$ TEASPOON CAYENNE PEPPER (OPTIONAL)

SALT TO TASTE

FLOUR FOR DREDGING

OLIVE OR PEANUT OIL FOR FRYING

LEMON WEDGES FOR SERVING

Cut the heads off the sardines, cut open along the belly, remove the innards, and remove the bones by pressing along the backbone to open each fish like a book, snapping off the bone just at the tail. Rinse and dry the fish.

To make the filling, cook the potatoes in salted water until tender, about 15 minutes. Drain and put through a ricer or mash. Mix in all the remaining ingredients.

Take 1 heaping tablespoon filling, flatten it into an oblong, and place it in between 2 opened-out sardines to make a "sandwich." Dredge in flour to coat both sides. In a large sauté pan or skillet, heat 2 inches oil over medium-high heat and fry the sardines in batches until golden on each side. Serve with lemon wedges.

Variation: In *Fleur de safran,* Jacqueline Cohen-Azuelos sandwiches filleted sardines with a paste of 3 minced cloves garlic, 2 tablespoons chopped fresh flat-leaf parsley, 2 tablespoons chopped fresh coriander (cilantro), 1 teaspoon sweet paprika, 1 tablespoon ground cumin, the juice of 1 lemon, and salt and pepper to taste. She dips them in flour and fries them in batches until golden.

: : : : : :

SAMAK HARRAH, *or*
POISSON *à la* CORIANDRE

FISH WITH FRESH CORIANDER

Fish and coriander are a classic pairing in the Southern Mediterranean. Slightly different versions of this dish appears in *La table juive,* attributed to Morocco, and in Anissa Helou's *Lebanese Cuisine.* This recipe is a composite as far as spicing goes, but the technique is Lebanese.

Serves 8

2 POUNDS FIRM FISH STEAKS OR FILLETS,
    SUCH AS HALIBUT, COD, OR SEA BASS
KOSHER SALT FOR SPRINKLING
8 TABLESPOONS OLIVE OIL
4 ONIONS, CHOPPED
1 1/2 CUPS CHOPPED FRESH CORIANDER (CILANTRO)
6 TO 10 CLOVES GARLIC, MINCED
1/2 TEASPOON FRESHLY GROUND BLACK PEPPER
1 TEASPOON GROUND CUMIN
1 TABLESPOON GROUND TURMERIC
3 OR 4 SMALL DRIED RED PEPPERS, OR 1/2 TEASPOON
    CAYENNE PEPPER
1/2 CUP FRESH LEMON JUICE
STEAMED RICE FOR SERVING

Rinse the fish and sprinkle with kosher salt. Cover and refrigerate for about 1 hour.

In a large sauté pan or skillet, heat 4 tablespoons of the oil over high heat and quickly sear the fish to color both sides. Drain and set aside.

Heat the remaining 4 tablespoons oil in the same pan and cook the onions until golden, about 15 minutes. Add the fresh coriander, garlic, and spices and sauté for a minute or two. Add the lemon juice and simmer until thickened, about 10 minutes. Arrange the fish on top of the sauce. Cover the pan and simmer over low heat until the fish is opaque throughout, about 5 minutes. Serve warm or at room temperature, with rice.

Variation: The Moroccan version of this dish has no onions but arranges half the chopped fresh coriander in a baking dish or large sauté pan or skillet. The fish fillets are placed on top. The garlic, pepper, cumin, turmeric, and crushed red peppers are combined in a small bowl and mixed with 1/2 cup oil. This is poured over the fish, 1 cup of water is added to the pan, and the rest of the fresh coriander is spread on top. It may be baked in a preheated 450 degree F oven or covered and cooked over low heat on the stovetop until the fish is opaque throughout, about 15 minutes. Serve with fresh fava beans and boiled new potatoes.

: : : : : :

SAMAK *bil* TAHINEH

FISH WITH TAHINI SAUCE

This is a classic fish dish from Syria and Lebanon. A whole fish is baked or grilled and skinned. It is coated with a garlicky lemon-laced tahini sauce and baked again. After cooking it is placed on a serving platter and decorated lavishly with cucumbers, radishes, pine nuts, pomegranate seeds, and so on. Usually served at room temperature, it could be the centerpiece of a summer buffet.

Serves 6

KOSHER SALT TO TASTE
ONE 3- TO 4-POUND WHOLE FISH, SUCH AS SNAPPER OR
    SEA BASS, OR 2$\frac{1}{2}$ POUNDS FIRM WHITE FISH FILLETS
2 TABLESPOONS FRESH LEMON JUICE
3 TABLESPOONS OLIVE OIL

For the tahini sauce:
$\frac{1}{4}$ CUP CANOLA OIL
2 TO 3 ONIONS, CHOPPED
3 TO 5 CLOVES GARLIC, MINCED
1 TEASPOON SALT
$\frac{1}{2}$ CUP TAHINI (SESAME PASTE)
6 TO 8 TABLESPOONS FRESH LEMON JUICE
6 TABLESPOONS COLD WATER OR FISH STOCK,
    OR MORE AS NEEDED
$\frac{1}{4}$ CUP PINE NUTS, TOASTED, FOR GARNISH
3 TABLESPOONS COARSELY CHOPPED FRESH
    FLAT-LEAF PARSLEY FOR GARNISH

Salt the whole fish inside and out, or both sides of the fillets, then rinse. Cut 3 or 4 slits on either side of the whole fish. Let rest for 30 minutes in the refrigerator. Sprinkle the whole fish or the fillets with the lemon juice and olive oil. Preheat the oven to 400 degrees F.

To make the sauce, in a medium sauté pan or skillet, heat the oil over medium heat and add the onions. Sauté for 10 minutes. Add the garlic and cook a few minutes longer. In a food processor, combine the onion mixture, salt, tahini, and lemon juice. Add cold water or fish stock as needed to make a fluffy mixture. Set aside.

Bake the whole fish for 20 minutes, then remove from the oven and peel away its skin. Place the fish or fish fillets in the baking pan and spread with the tahini mixture. Bake until opaque throughout, basting with pan juices occasionally, about 25 minutes. Transfer to a serving platter. Serve warm or at room temperature, garnished with the toasted pine nuts and parsley.

: : : : : :

KIBBEH SAMAK

FISH KIBBEH

Most people think of *kibbeh* as torpedo-shaped croquettes made with meat and bulgur wheat. This interesting layered version of *kibbeh* uses fish and is served in Syria and Southern Lebanon. The orange zest, fresh coriander, and black pepper provide a flavor boost for what could otherwise be a bland dish.

Serves 6

2^1/$_2$ CUPS FINE BULGUR WHEAT

1^1/$_2$ POUNDS WHITE FISH FILLETS, SUCH AS SOLE, COD,
     OR HALIBUT, CHOPPED

1 LARGE ONION, CHOPPED

^{1}/$_4$ CUP CHOPPED FRESH CORIANDER (CILANTRO)

^{1}/$_4$ CUP CHOPPED FRESH FLAT-LEAF PARSLEY

GRATED ZEST OF 1 LARGE ORANGE

3 TEASPOONS KOSHER SALT

FRESHLY GROUND BLACK PEPPER TO TASTE

For the filling:

^{1}/$_4$ CUP OLIVE OIL

^{1}/$_3$ CUP PINE NUTS

2 LARGE ONIONS, DICED

SALT AND FRESHLY GROUND BLACK PEPPER TO TASTE

^{1}/$_3$ CUP OLIVE OIL OR MELTED UNSALTED BUTTER

Oil a 9-by-12-inch baking dish. Put the bulgur in a sieve and rinse under cold water for a few minutes. Drain well and press out the moisture with the back of a large spoon. Set aside.

In food processor, combine the fish and onion. Pulse to combine. Quickly pulse in the fresh coriander, parsley, and orange zest, then the bulgur. Add the salt and pepper. Knead well to blend. Set aside. (You might want to fry a small patty to test the seasoning.)

To make the filling, in a medium sauté pan or skillet, heat the oil over low heat and toast the pine nuts. Using a slotted spoon, transfer to a plate. Add the onions to the pan and cook over medium heat for about 8 minutes. Season with salt and pepper. Return the pine nuts to the pan.

Preheat the oven to 350 degrees F. Pat half the fish mixture into the prepared baking dish. Spread all of the onion mixture over the fish layer. Top with the remaining fish mixture and spread it evenly. Cut through into diamond shapes with a sharp knife. Pour the olive oil or melted butter over the top and bake until golden brown, 30 to 35 minutes. Serve hot or at room temperature.

Variation: For the fish *kibbeh* in *From the Land of Figs and Olives,* omit the filling and grind 1 pound chopped fish, 1 cup soaked and drained bulgur, 1 chopped onion, 2 cloves garlic, ^{1}/$_4$ cup chopped fresh coriander (cilantro), 2 tablespoons flour, ^{1}/$_4$ teaspoon *each* ground cinnamon, nutmeg, and allspice, and 1^1/$_2$ teaspoons salt to a paste in a food processor. Form into patties and fry in ^{1}/$_2$ inch olive oil over medium-high heat until golden. Serve with a sauce of pureed garlic, lemon juice, and olive oil.

: : : : : :

THON *à la* TOMATE

TUNA WITH TOMATOES

This Moroccan recipe for tuna could also be prepared with cod, snapper, or another firm white fish. Leone Jaffin's Algerian version omits preserved lemon and adds 2 small hot red peppers and a few rinsed capers. She fries the fish briefly to color it, then braises it covered with the sauce and serves the fish with steamed potatoes. Keep in mind that in the Mediterranean, tuna is not served rare; all recipes using this meaty fish cook it until opaque throughout.

Serves 4

4 THICK 6-OUNCE SLICES TUNA OR ANOTHER FIRM FISH

$1/3$ CUP NO. 1 CHERMOULA (PAGE 108), OR SALT AND
   FRESH LEMON JUICE FOR SPRINKLING

3 CUPS CANNED CHOPPED TOMATOES WITH JUICE

2 CLOVES GARLIC, MINCED

$1/4$ CUP CHOPPED FRESH FLAT-LEAF PARSLEY

PEEL OF 1 PRESERVED LEMON (PAGE 50), CUT INTO
   THIN SLIVERS

$1/4$ TEASPOON CAYENNE PEPPER, OR TO TASTE

12 OIL-CURED BLACK OLIVES (OPTIONAL)

2 TABLESPOONS CAPERS, RINSED (OPTIONAL)

If you have time, put the fish in a large casserole, coat it with the chermoula, cover, and refrigerate for 4 hours. This step may be omitted, but it adds a lot of flavor to the fish. If you are pressed for time, just sprinkle fish with salt and lemon juice and marinate at room temperature for a half hour.

Put the tomatoes in a medium saucepan and cook over medium heat, stirring often, until they have been reduced to a thick puree, adding the garlic during the last few minutes. Stir in the parsley, lemon peel, and cayenne, and olives and capers, if using. Simmer for 5 minutes.

Preheat the oven to 400 degrees F. Remove the fish from the refrigerator. Place fish in an oiled baking dish and cover with tomato sauce. Cover the dish with aluminum foil and bake until the fish is opaque throughout, about 20 minutes. Serve hot or cold.

Variation: Dip the slices of tuna in flour and fry quickly in oil until browned. Pour the tomato sauce over, cover, and braise over low heat until the fish is opaque throughout, about 20 minutes.

: : : : : :

POULTRY

chapter 6

POULTRY

Once upon a time in the Mediterranean, chicken was more costly than meat, and hens were considered especially valuable for the many eggs they supplied and that were used throughout the year in a myriad of dishes. Chicken was served on the Sabbath and at holidays, and still is. It is the signature dish for Yom Kippur because of the custom of *kapparoth,* where a chicken is slaughtered as a symbolic sacrifice for every member of the family. Chicken is used in stews as a lighter and more elegant alternative to meat. Algerians prefer braised chicken with their couscous. Many birds, such as turkeys, pigeon, and small chickens, are stuffed with meat and grains for a festive presentation. Sauces might be sweetened by the addition of honey or fruits, or caramelized onions cooked to a confit. Or they might be savory, with spiced onions, preserved lemons, and briny cured olives. Poultry is the basis of a spectacular holiday pastry, *b'stilla* (see page 57). It is also paired with noodles for a homey family meal, ground for meatballs, baked into a sturdy meat loaf, and added to omelets and soups to make them more substantial.

DJEJ MACARUNI ★ SYRIAN CHICKEN WITH MACARONI

DJEJ MACARUNI

SYRIAN CHICKEN WITH MACARONI

According to Gilda Angel, this is a Sabbath favorite
of the Syrian Jews. It is called *treya* in Egypt, and
a version of chicken and noodles appears in the
Moroccan kitchen as *inetria*. Both words are related
to the early Arabic name for pasta, which was *itriya*.
These combos of chicken and noodles are simple
and comforting. Certainly this dish would more
than please children and any fussy eaters in your
family. It's the beloved chicken and pasta dish they
hunger for. You could use leftover roast turkey or
chicken for this dish, too.

Serves 4 TO 6

2 SMALL BROILER CHICKENS, CUT INTO SERVING PIECES
SALT AND FRESHLY GROUND BLACK PEPPER TO TASTE
SWEET PAPRIKA TO TASTE
2 TO 3 CLOVES GARLIC, MINCED
1 POUND MACARONI
2 TABLESPOONS OLIVE OIL
$^2/_3$ CUP TOMATO SAUCE
$^1/_2$ CUP CHICKEN BROTH
$^1/_2$ TEASPOON GROUND CINNAMON
$^1/_2$ TEASPOON GROUND ALLSPICE

Preheat the oven to 375 degrees F. Season the chicken
pieces with salt, pepper, paprika, and garlic. Put the
pieces in a baking pan. Cover with a lid or aluminum
foil and bake until very tender, about $1^1/_2$ hours.

Cook the pasta in salted boiling water until al dente
and drain. Rinse with cold water to stop the cooking.
Toss with the olive oil to prevent sticking.

Remove the chicken from the pan and let cool to the
touch. Remove all the skin and carefully remove the
meat from the bones. Add the pasta to the pan and
toss it in the pan juices. Add the tomato sauce, broth,
and spices and mix well. Add the chicken to the pasta.
Bake, uncovered, for 45 minutes, or until golden and
crispy. Serve hot.

Moroccan Variation from Simy Danan: Cook
a cut-up 4-pound chicken in 6 cups of broth or
water flavored with 1 teaspoon ground turmeric or
$^1/_2$ teaspoon saffron threads, 2 teaspoons salt, and
$^1/_2$ teaspoon freshly ground black pepper until very
tender. Remove the chicken from the broth and let
cool to the touch. Skin and bone the chicken. Cook
$^3/_4$ pound fresh egg noodles in the chicken broth
until tender. Top the noodles with the chicken.

: : : : : :

TERRINE *de* POULET

ALGERIAN CHICKEN AND MEAT PÂTÉ

The recipe for this chicken and meat loaf comes
from *La table juive*. It can be served warm but is
excellent at room temperature, making it an ideal
dish for the Sabbath. While not traditional, you
could serve it with a tomato sauce (page 156) or a
puree of roasted red peppers seasoned with lemon
and fresh coriander (cilantro).

Serves 6

BAY LEAVES FOR LINING, PLUS 2 TO 3 BAY LEAVES
ONE 3$^1/_2$-POUND CHICKEN, SKINNED AND BONED, OR
   1 POUND GROUND CHICKEN AND 2 SMALL SKINLESS,
     BONELESS CHICKEN BREAST HALVES
1 POUND GROUND BEEF OR VEAL

2 EGGS, LIGHTLY BEATEN

SALT AND FRESHLY GROUND BLACK PEPPER TO TASTE

$^1/_2$ TEASPOON FRESHLY GRATED NUTMEG

$^1/_4$ CUP CHOPPED FRESH FLAT-LEAF PARSLEY

$^1/_4$ CUP CHOPPED FRESH MINT

2 TEASPOONS CHOPPED FRESH THYME

1 ONION, FINELY CHOPPED

6 CLOVES GARLIC, MINCED

Preheat the oven to 350 degrees F. Oil a 4-cup mold or loaf pan. Line the bottom with bay leaves.

Reserve the breast fillets. Finely chop the rest of the chicken and combine it or the ground chicken with the beef or veal. In a small bowl, combine all the remaining ingredients except the bay leaves and chicken breasts and mix well. Stir into the chicken mixture until blended. Fry up a sample of this mixture, or poach it in a little stock or water, to test the seasoning. Adjust as needed.

Pat half of the meat mixture into the prepared mold. Add the reserved breasts and top with remaining meat mixture. Top with 2 to 3 bay leaves and cover the mold with oiled aluminum foil. Bake for 1$^1/_4$ hours. Let rest for 10 minutes, then unmold. Serve warm or at room temperature, cut into slices.

: : : : : :

DAR LAARCH, *or* BOULETTES *de* POULET DITES *la* MARIÉE

THE BRIDE'S CHICKEN MEATBALLS

Chicken meatballs can be a wonderful weeknight supper, served with rice or couscous. In Tunisia, Daisy Taieb's family served chicken meatballs seasoned with crushed dried rose petals to break the fast after Yom Kippur. If you can't find dried rose petals, the chicken balls will still be delicious.

Serves 6 TO 8

For the meatballs:

2 POUNDS GROUND CHICKEN

4 SMALL ONIONS, FINELY CHOPPED

$^1/_4$ CUP CHOPPED FRESH FLAT-LEAF PARSLEY

6 TABLESPOONS CHOPPED FRESH CORIANDER (CILANTRO)

2 CLOVES GARLIC, MINCED

FOUR 1-INCH-THICK SLICES COUNTRY BREAD, SOAKED IN
   WATER AND SQUEEZED DRY

3 TEASPOONS CRUSHED DRIED UNSPRAYED ROSE PETALS
   (OPTIONAL)

FRESHLY GRATED NUTMEG TO TASTE

GOOD PINCH OF GROUND TURMERIC OR SAFFRON
   THREADS, CRUSHED

2 TEASPOONS SALT

FRESHLY GROUND BLACK PEPPER TO TASTE

2 EGGS

For the sauce:

2 TABLESPOONS OLIVE OIL

4 LARGE TOMATOES, PEELED, SEEDED, AND CHOPPED

2 CLOVES GARLIC, MINCED

1 BAY LEAF

SALT AND FRESHLY GROUND BLACK PEPPER TO TASTE

1/2 TEASPOON GROUND TURMERIC, OR 1/4 TEASPOON
   SAFFRON THREADS, CRUSHED

COUSCOUS FOR SERVING (PAGE 83)

To make the meatballs, in a large bowl, combine all the ingredients and knead the mixture until it holds together. Form one meatball and poach it in lightly salted water to test the seasoning. Adjust as necessary. Form the mixture into walnut-sized balls.

To make the sauce, in a large sauté pan or skillet, heat the oil over medium-high heat. Add all the remaining ingredients and about 2 inches of water. Cook for 5 minutes. Add the chicken balls, cover, and poach until cooked through, 15 to 20 minutes. If you like, brown them under the broiler or in a hot oven. Serve with couscous alongside or in the center of a platter, surrounded by the meatballs.

: : : : : :

ESTOFADO
ROAST CHICKEN WITH EGGPLANT AND ONION CONFIT

Estofado is a very old Judeo-Spanish dish where chicken is combined with a twice-cooked sweetened eggplant compote. This recipe comes from *Saveurs de mon enfance* and is a specialty of Tangier and Tetouan. *La table juive* calls this *baraniya* and adds chickpeas to the eggplant and onion confit. For another version of *baraniya,* see the eggplant confit on page 162.

Serves 8

2 SMALL BROILER CHICKENS, EACH CUT INTO
   SERVING PIECES

SALT AND FRESHLY GROUND BLACK PEPPER TO TASTE

1 1/4 CUPS OLIVE OIL, OR AS NEEDED

5 POUNDS GLOBE EGGPLANTS, CUT INTO
   1/3-INCH-THICK SLICES

5 POUNDS ONIONS, CHOPPED

1 CUP SUGAR

1 TEASPOON GROUND CINNAMON

1 TEASPOON RAS AL HANOUT (PAGE 49; OPTIONAL)

1/2 CUP WATER

Preheat the oven to 375 degrees F. Rinse the chicken pieces, dry well, and sprinkle with salt and pepper. Place the chicken pieces on an oiled flat rack in a large roasting pan and roast until the juices run clear when the chicken is pierced, about 35 minutes.

In a large sauté pan or skillet, heat 1/4 cup of the oil over medium-high heat and sauté the sliced eggplant in batches until golden, adding oil as needed. Set aside.

Add the remaining 1 cup oil to a large sauté pan or skillet over low heat and add the chopped onions, sugar, salt, pepper, cinnamon, and ras al hanout, if using. Cook, stirring occasionally, until the onions are caramelized and thickened, about 20 minutes.

In a large Dutch oven, make a layer of one third of the onions, then one third of the eggplant. Repeat to use the remaining onion mixture and eggplant. Add the chicken. Add the water to the pan. Cover and simmer for 1 hour, or until chicken is very tender.

: : : : : :

POULET *aux* COINGS

ALGERIAN TAGINE OF CHICKEN WITH QUINCE

Leone Jaffin, in her book *150 recettes et mille et un souvenirs d'une juive d'Algérie,* recommends this fragrant stew of chicken and quince as the ideal dish for Rosh Hashanah. In Joelle Bahloul's family, it was eaten the night before the Yom Kippur fast. Quince are thought by some to have been the apple in the Garden of Eden. When they are in season, they add a perfumed sweetness to any dish. Ideally, they should cook until their Venetian red color comes up. I've noticed that most European quinces turn red quickly, but ours become tender well before they take on color. As added insurance you may want to add a bit of pomegranate molasses to the poaching liquid. If you are making quince preserves (page 161), you can cook them for a long time, as texture is not a factor; however, if you want the quince slices to retain their shape, you cannot cook them too long. Because of this I prefer to cook the quince separately, then add them to the chicken stew during the last 20 minutes of braising. That way every part of the dish is well cooked and not mushy.

Serves 6

2 POUNDS QUINCE, PEELED AND CUT INTO EIGHTHS

POMEGRANATE MOLASSES AS NEEDED

$1/2$ CUP PEANUT OIL

1 LARGE CHICKEN OR 2 BROILERS, CUT INTO SERVING
    PIECES ($4 1/2$ TO 5 POUNDS TOTAL)

3 ONIONS, CHOPPED

$1/2$ TEASPOON FRESHLY GRATED NUTMEG

2 TEASPOONS GROUND CINNAMON

SALT TO TASTE

Cook the quince in simmering water to cover until they are tender and have turned pink, 35 to 45 minutes. Set aside in their poaching liquid. Add a bit of pomegranate molasses if the color has not come up.

In a large sauté pan or skillet, heat the oil over high heat and brown the chicken pieces on all sides. Set aside. In the fat remaining in the pan, sauté the onions over medium heat until golden, 15 to 20 minutes. Stir in the spices and cook 5 minutes longer. Add the chicken and its accumulated juices, cover the pan, and braise the chicken for about 20 minutes. Add the cooked quince and some of the quince liquids. Simmer 15 minutes longer, or until the chicken is tender. Season with salt and add more spice, if you like.

Variation: This dish also can be made with 3 pounds of cubed lamb shoulder. Brown the meat in oil, cook the onions and spices in oil, and braise the two together in a bit of water or broth until the meat is tender. Stir in the cooked quince and some of the quince liquids and cook for 15 or 20 minutes. This stew might require more seasoning, as lamb is more intense in flavor than chicken.

Note: If you can't find quince, you may make this with apples.

: : : : : :

DINDE FARCI

STUFFED TURKEY

This recipe comes from Viviane Moryoussef. Instead of stuffing the cavity of the bird, the mixture is piped under the skin. You may use this technique with poussins or a large roasting chicken. The stuffing would be good inside smaller birds, too.

Serves 6 TO 8

1 POUND WHOLE FRESH CHESTNUTS
ONE 8-POUND TURKEY

For the stuffing:
$1/2$ POUND GROUND VEAL
$3/4$ POUND GROUND BEEF
2 HARD-COOKED EGGS, CHOPPED
1 CUP FRESH BREAD CRUMBS
$1^1/_2$ TO $1^3/_4$ CUPS CHOPPED COOKED CHESTNUTS
6 TABLESPOONS CHOPPED FRESH FLAT-LEAF PARSLEY
SALT AND FRESHLY GROUND BLACK PEPPER TO TASTE
1 TEASPOON *EACH* GROUND MACE AND CINNAMON
3 EGGS, BEATEN
2 TABLESPOONS OLIVE OIL

For the basting sauce:
$2/_3$ CUP OLIVE OIL
JUICES OF 1 LEMON AND 1 ORANGE
1 TEASPOON SALT
1 TEASPOON FRESHLY GROUND BLACK PEPPER
$1/2$ TEASPOON SAFFRON THREADS, CRUSHED

1 CUP CHICKEN BROTH
PINCH OF CRUSHED SAFFRON THREADS

Cut an X on the flat side of each chestnut. Cook the chestnuts in a pan of boiling water for 5 minutes. Peel off the shells and inner skins while hot. Set aside.

Rinse the bird well inside and out. Carefully and gently slip your fingers under the skin and loosen from the meat, taking care not to tear it.

In a large bowl, combine all of the ingredients for the stuffing except the eggs and oil. Work in the eggs and oil with your hands to make a smooth paste. Or, pulse everything together in a food processor.

With the aid of a pastry bag, push this stuffing between the skin and the flesh of the bird. Sew up the openings. Pat the stuffing to distribute it evenly. Truss the bird, if you like.

In a small saucepan, combine all the basting sauce ingredients and heat over low heat for 5 minutes.

Preheat the oven to 350 degrees F. Brush the turkey generously with the basting sauce and place on an oiled rack in a roasting pan. Add a bit of water to the pan. Roast until the bird is golden, about 2 hours and 30 minutes, basting often with the sauce and pan juices. Test for doneness by piercing the thigh with a knife; when the juices run clear, the bird is done. Remove from oven and transfer to a carving board. Let rest for 10 minutes.

In a saucepan, heat the chicken broth and saffron. Add the peeled whole chestnuts and simmer until tender but not falling apart, 8 to 10 minutes. Carve the turkey and place the slices on a platter. Arrange the chestnuts on the platter around the turkey.

: : : : : :

PIGEONS FARCIS *de* VIANDE *et* RAISINS SECS

SQUABS STUFFED WITH MEAT AND RAISINS

Fortunée Hazan-Arama's squab recipe from *Saveurs de mon enfance* is a specialty of Fez and Rabat. She uses large black raisins with seeds, then removes the seeds. Let's be lazy and use seedless raisins. She also grinds the meat through a meat chopper, but we can combine the entire stuffing in a food processor.

Serves 4

4 SQUABS (ABOUT 1 POUND EACH)

SALT TO TASTE

1 TEASPOON GROUND GINGER

5 TABLESPOONS OLIVE OIL

2 ONIONS, FINELY CHOPPED

1 TABLESPOON SUGAR

FRESHLY GROUND BLACK PEPPER TO TASTE

$^1/_4$ TEASPOON FRESHLY GRATED NUTMEG

$^3/_4$ CUP BLANCHED ALMONDS

$1^1/_4$ CUPS SEEDLESS RAISINS

$^3/_4$ POUND GROUND BEEF

Rinse the squabs and pat dry. Rub the insides with salt and $^1/_2$ teaspoon of the ginger.

In a large sauté pan or skillet, heat 2 tablespoons of the oil over medium heat and cook half of the onions until tender, about 8 minutes. Add the sugar, salt, pepper, and $^1/_8$ teaspoon of the nutmeg. Cook a few minutes more, then set aside.

In a food processor, chop the almonds and $^3/_4$ cup of the raisins with short pulses. Add the beef and cooked onions and pulse quickly to combine. Stuff the squabs with this mixture.

In the same pan, heat 2 tablespoons of the oil over medium heat and sauté the remaining chopped onions until golden. Add the remaining $^1/_8$ teaspoon nutmeg and $^1/_2$ teaspoon ginger and cook for a minute or two. Set aside.

Add the remaining 1 tablespoon oil to the pan and brown the squab on all sides. Return the onions to the pan and add water to almost cover the onions. Cover and braise for 20 minutes. Add the remaining $^1/_2$ cup raisins, and cook until tender, about 15 more minutes. Transfer the squab to a serving platter. Cook the sauce over medium heat to reduce. Taste and adjust the seasoning. Spoon the sauce over the birds and serve with couscous.

Variation: Pigeons des Mariées (Squabs for Newlyweds) Stuff squabs with meat; cooked rice; onions; a mixture of dried fruits, such as apricots, raisins, and prunes; sweet spices such as ginger, cinnamon, and mace; and some black pepper. Braise with onions, almonds, raisins, saffron, and honey (see Mrouzia, page 145) to wish the newlyweds a sweet life together.

: : : : : :

POULET FARCI *avec* COUSCOUS *aux* OLIVES *et* CITRONS CONFITS

COUSCOUS-STUFFED CHICKEN WITH OLIVES AND PRESERVED LEMONS

I love the classic Moroccan dish of chicken with preserved lemon and olives. But this version from *Saveurs de mon enfance* is even more intriguing, with its couscous and almond stuffing. Casablanca and Marrakech are the cities where this dish is most popular.

Serves 4

1 LARGE CHICKEN (4 TO 5 POUNDS), OR 4 POUSSINS OR
  CORNISH HENS
1 LEMON, HALVED
SALT FOR SPRINKLING
1 CUP COUSCOUS
³/₄ CUP SALTED WATER
2 TABLESPOONS OLIVE OIL
²/₃ CUP BLANCHED ALMONDS, TOASTED AND CHOPPED
¹/₄ TEASPOON SAFFRON THREADS, CRUSHED AND
  STEEPED IN 2 TABLESPOONS HOT WATER
¹/₂ TEASPOON GROUND CINNAMON
¹/₂ TEASPOON GINGER

For the sauce:
¹/₄ CUP OLIVE OIL
2 LARGE ONIONS, CHOPPED
2 SMALL HOT RED PEPPERS
¹/₂ TEASPOON GROUND GINGER
¹/₂ TEASPOON SAFFRON THREADS, CRUSHED AND
  STEEPED IN 2 TABLESPOONS HOT WATER
SALT AND FRESHLY GROUND BLACK PEPPER TO TASTE
1 WHOLE HEAD GARLIC
1 LARGE BUNCH FRESH CORIANDER (CILANTRO)

2 CUPS WATER
4 CUPS (1 POUND) CRACKED GREEN OLIVES
4 SMALL PRESERVED LEMONS (PAGE 50),
  CUT INTO QUARTERS

Rinse the chicken well inside and out. Pat dry. Rub with lemon halves and sprinkle with salt inside and out.

Put the couscous in a steamer basket. Sprinkle the couscous with the water and steam over boiling water for 10 minutes. Toss with the oil and steam again for 10 to 15 minutes. Remove from heat and let cool slightly. Fold in the almonds and spices. Stuff into the bird(s). Or for quick couscous, put the couscous in a saucepan. Bring the water to a boil and stir in the spices. Pour over the couscous and cover with aluminum foil. Let rest for 10 minutes, then fluff with a fork. Fold in the almonds.

In a large, deep saucepan, heat the oil over medium heat and sauté the onions until tender, about 8 minutes. Add the red peppers, ginger, saffron, salt, and pepper. Cook for a few minutes. Add the birds(s) to the pan and brown on all sides, turning often. Add the garlic, fresh coriander, and water. Cover the pan and simmer until tender, about 1 hour for small birds and 1¹/₂ hours for a large bird. During the last 15 minutes, add the olives and preserved lemons.

Uncover the pan and cook to reduce the sauce. Taste and adjust the seasoning. Discard the garlic, peppers, and coriander. Transfer the chicken to a platter. Cut a large bird into serving pieces or quarters; cut smaller birds in half. Spoon the sauce around the bird(s) and garnish with the lemons and olives.

: : : : : :

DJEJ MIHSHEE *bi* ROZ (*bi* BURGHUL)

ROAST CHICKEN STUFFED WITH RICE (OR BULGUR)

In Syria and Lebanon, chickens are stuffed with a fragrant rice pilaf. If there is no rice in the house, bulgur may be used. Both make a delicious filling. The grain is not cooked completely, as it will continue to cook inside the birds and absorb the meat juices.

Serves 6

6 CORNISH HENS OR POUSSINS (ABOUT 1^1/$_2$ POUNDS
    EACH), OR 1 LARGE ROASTING CHICKEN OR CAPON
1 LEMON, HALVED
KOSHER SALT FOR SPRINKLING

For the stuffing:
2^1/$_2$ CUPS WATER, LIGHTLY SALTED
1^1/$_2$ CUPS BASMATI RICE OR BULGUR WHEAT
^{1}/$_4$ CUP OLIVE OIL OR MARGARINE
2 ONIONS, DICED
1 TEASPOON GROUND ALLSPICE
1 TEASPOON GROUND CINNAMON
^{2}/$_3$ CUP DRIED CURRANTS, SOAKED IN HOT WATER
    UNTIL PLUMP, THEN DRAINED
^{1}/$_2$ CUP PINE NUTS, TOASTED
^{1}/$_2$ CUP ALMONDS, TOASTED
^{1}/$_4$ CUP CHOPPED FRESH FLAT-LEAF PARSLEY
2 TABLESPOONS GRATED LEMON ZEST (OPTIONAL)
SALT AND FRESHLY GROUND BLACK PEPPER TO TASTE

For the basting mixture:
4 TO 6 TABLESPOONS OLIVE OIL OR MELTED MARGARINE
^{1}/$_2$ TEASPOON GROUND ALLSPICE
2 CLOVES GARLIC, MINCED
3 TABLESPOONS FRESH LEMON JUICE
SALT AND FRESHLY GROUND BLACK PEPPER TO TASTE

Rinse the birds well inside and out and pat dry. Rub with the lemon halves inside and out, then sprinkle with salt.

To make the stuffing, in a medium saucepan, bring the salted water to a boil. Add the rice or bulgur and stir once. Reduce heat to a simmer, cover, and cook for about 15 minutes, or until most of the liquid is absorbed. Set aside.

In a medium sauté pan or skillet, heat the oil or melt the margarine over medium heat. Add the onions and cook until tender, about 8 minutes. Add the allspice and cinnamon and cook for a few minutes longer.

Combine the grain, onion mixture, drained currants, nuts, parsley, and lemon zest, if using. Add salt and pepper. Stuff into the birds.

To make the basting mixture, in a small saucepan, combine all the ingredients.

Preheat the oven to 400 degrees F. Place the birds on a rack in a roasting pan. Roast until juices run clear when a thigh is pierced and the legs wiggle easily, 45 to 60 minutes, basting occasionally with the basting mixture. Let rest for a few minutes, then serve 1 whole hen or poussin per guest, or cut the birds in half to serve. Carve a large chicken in the usual fashion. Serving the stuffing on the side.

Variation: The stuffing is called *hashwa* if ground meat is added to the grain mixture.

: : : : : :

MEATS

chapter 7

MEATS

For centuries, meat was served only on special occasions in the Mediterranean. Most people were too poor to eat it regularly. This was certainly the case with the Sephardic Jews. On the Sabbath and holidays, meat dishes were joyfully anticipated and eaten with great appreciation. Lamb and what today we'd call mutton were most commonly available. However, mutton is strong in flavor and aroma, so it gradually lost prestige, and the more costly beef and veal gained a place on the table. Today, everyone eats meat, and beef is served more often than lamb, although to my palate, lamb takes on spices and the sweetness of fruit in a more balanced way.

Most of the Sabbath meat dishes took the form of a *d'fina,* a one-pot stew that was cooked ever so slowly in the embers of a dying fire, either on the home brazier or in the baker's communal oven. These stews could be simply meat with beans and eggs in their shells, or they might have grains, a meat loaf, potatoes, and/or dried fruits added for an extra touch. The most festive meat stews had fruit and nuts, and were sweetened with honey. In the spirit of economy, meatballs were creatively presented as stuffings in vegetables, braised atop tomatoes, sauced with onion confit or in a saffron-tinged sauce, or wrapped around skewers and grilled as kefta. Some meatballs or stews were extended with vegetables and served with couscous, wheat, rice, barley, or during Passover, matzoh. At large family celebrations, a whole lamb was grilled on the spit and served with an assortment of vegetable salads.

D'FINA *and* SKHINA

SABBATH STEW

In the Orthodox Jewish tradition, it is forbidden to light a fire or work on the Sabbath. In order to have a midday meal on Saturday, housewives put one-pot stews in a very low oven or the oven of the local baker before sundown on Friday and keep it there until lunch the next day. In Spain these stews are called *cocido,* in France *cassoulet,* and in other parts of Europe *cholent. D'fina* is a typical Sabbath stew. Joelle Bahloul, in her wonderful book *The Architecture of Memory*, tells of Jewish life in Algeria. Of *d'fina* she says, "Its flavor and thick consistency are presented as the gustatory representation of Sabbath time in abeyance."

The name comes from the Arabic *dfi'ne,* which means "buried"; in this case, the cooking pot was buried in the fireplace ashes. Eggs in their shells are also buried in the stew, much like *hamin* eggs (eggs cooked for many hours with brown onion skins), and they have a similar creamy texture. *D'fina* can also be served at Passover, when chickpeas are replaced by fresh fava beans or peas. And for breaking the fast at Yom Kippur, *d'fina* is made with chicken, usually stuffed with a meat mixture sweetened with almond and cinnamon.

In Morocco, this dish may be called *dafina* or *adafina,* but it becomes a *skhina* (which means "hot") when sweet potatoes, roasted barley or rice, and sometimes a meat loaf seasoned with sweet spices are added to the pot and cooked along with the basic stew of meat, chickpeas, potatoes, and eggs. One hour before the meal is to be served, the top of the pot is removed so that the stew may brown. Leftovers are eaten at room temperature. When I was last in Morocco, I was invited to a reception given by the American consul. He and his wife, both of them Jewish, served a Moroccan Jewish banquet. The *skhina* with barley was the star.

Serves 8, or 8 TO 10 for variations

Egyptian D'fina:

2 TABLESPOONS OLIVE OIL

2 LARGE ONIONS, CHOPPED

6 CLOVES GARLIC, MINCED

3 TO 4 POUNDS STEWING BEEF OR BRISKET, CUBED

6 POTATOES, PEELED AND HALVED IF LARGE

$1\frac{1}{2}$ CUPS DRIED CHICKPEAS, SOAKED OVERNIGHT
    AND DRAINED

1 TEASPOON GINGER

1 TEASPOON GROUND ALLSPICE

SALT AND FRESHLY GROUND BLACK PEPPER TO TASTE

WATER OR BROTH TO COVER

8 EGGS, IN THEIR SHELLS, RINSED

Preheat the oven to 250 degrees F. In a large, heavy Dutch oven, heat the oil over medium heat and cook the onions until golden, 15 to 20 minutes. Add all the remaining ingredients. Bring to a boil and reduce heat to a simmer. Cover and bake for 8 hours, or until the meat and chickpeas are tender. (Or, bake at 300 degrees F for 4 to 5 hours.) This stew could also be simmered over very low heat on top of the stove. To serve, peel the eggs and return them to the stew.

Variation: Moroccan Skhina Add 12 dates or dried apricots to the above stew when adding the liquids. Prepare the following Moroccan meat loaf (sometimes called *kora*): Combine $\frac{3}{4}$ pound ground chuck, $\frac{1}{2}$ cup fresh bread crumbs, $\frac{1}{2}$ teaspoon ground mace or nutmeg, salt and freshly ground black pepper to taste, 2 beaten eggs, 2 tablespoons olive oil, and $\frac{1}{4}$ cup chopped fresh flat-leaf parsley. Mix well, form into a long loaf, wrap in cheesecloth, and tie the ends. Place in the pot and cook along with the meat and chickpeas. To serve, unwrap and offer along with the stew.

Sweet Potato Variation: Peel and cut 1 pound sweet potatoes into large chunks. Rub with a paste of 1 beaten egg, 3 tablespoons sugar, 1/2 teaspoon ground cinnamon, a pinch of cloves, and 1/2 cup ground almonds. Wrap in cheesecloth and tie. Add to the pot. To serve, unwrap and offer along with the stew.

Grain Variation: Rinse 2 cups cracked wheat, barley, or rice well and mix with 6 minced cloves garlic, 1 teaspoon sweet paprika, 1/2 teaspoon cayenne pepper, 1 teaspoon ground cumin, and 1/3 cup olive oil. Tie in cheesecloth and add to the pot. To serve, unwrap and offer along with the stew.

: : : : : :

T'FINA *aux* EPINARDS, *or* PKHAILA

TUNISIAN BEAN AND BEEF STEW WITH SPINACH ESSENCE

In Tunisia, *pkhaila* is served during Rosh Hashanah. This recipe is based on a dish served at the home of Daisy Taieb, author of *Les fêtes juives à Tunis racontées à mes filles.* Some families add *osbane,* a spicy sausage (page 140) after the meat has cooked for 1 hour. Others add a meat loaf in the manner of the *skhina* recipe (page 136). The Taieb family serves this with homemade semolina bread rather than couscous or rice. In Claudia Roden's version of this recipe, she wilts the spinach in oil, but others wilt it dry and cook it down without any oil at all.

Serves 6

2 1/2 POUNDS SPINACH, STEMMED

1 BUNCH FRESH CORIANDER (CILANTRO), STEMMED

1 CUP DRIED WHITE BEANS, SOAKED OVERNIGHT AND DRAINED

2 VEAL BONES

1 POUND BEEF BRISKET, CUT INTO 2-INCH PIECES

4 TO 6 CLOVES GARLIC

1 ONION, FINELY CHOPPED

1 CINNAMON STICK

1 TEASPOON HARISSA (PAGE 48)

3 TABLESPOONS CHOPPED FRESH DILL

3 TABLESPOONS CHOPPED FRESH MINT, OR 1 TABLESPOON DRIED MINT

3 QUARTS WATER

Rinse the spinach and fresh coriander well. In a large covered pot, cook the spinach and coriander over medium heat until wilted, about 3 to 5 minutes. Drain well and return to the pot. Cook over low heat, turning with a wooden spoon, until dry and browned, 20 to 30 minutes. Add the beans, veal bones, beef, garlic, onion, cinnamon stick, harissa, dill, mint, and water. Bring to a boil, reduce heat to a simmer, cover, and cook until the liquid is absorbed and the oil comes to the top of the dish, about 3 hours. Add more water if the dish becomes too dry while cooking.

Variation: Add *osbane* (page 140) after about 1 hour of cooking.

: : : : : :

MSOKI

TUNISIAN PASSOVER STEW
WITH SPRING VEGETABLES

If ever a dish were a celebration of spring, this one is. Andrée Zana-Murat and Daisy Taieb both offer a fabulous assortment of vegetables enhanced with the richness of meat juices and bits of cooked meat. It's like a giant minestrone. Zana-Murat adds *osbane* (page 140) to the stew after an hour or so of cooking. Crumbled matzoh is added at the end to absorb the fragrant juices. Reserve the lamb bone for the Passover plate.

Serves 10 TO 12

2 POUNDS FAVA BEANS, SHELLED

1 OR 2 CARDOONS, TRIMMED OF STRINGS, CUT INTO
    1-INCH PIECES, AND PARBOILED IN LEMON WATER
    FOR 5 MINUTES

8 CARROTS, DICED

1 SMALL SAVOY CABBAGE, CORED AND CUT INTO
    1¼-INCH PIECES

4 TURNIPS, DICED

½ HEAD YOUNG CELERY WITH LEAVES, DICED

1 CELERY ROOT, PEELED AND DICED

1 BULB FENNEL WITH LEAVES, DICED

2 TABLESPOONS GROUND DRIED UNSPRAYED
    ROSE PETALS (OPTIONAL)

2 TEASPOONS GROUND CORIANDER

1 TEASPOON FRESHLY GROUND PEPPER

8 CLOVES GARLIC, MINCED

3 WHITE ONIONS, DICED

1 TEASPOON SALT

8 TABLESPOONS CHOPPED FRESH CORIANDER (CILANTRO)

½ CUP CHOPPED FRESH DILL

½ CUP CHOPPED FRESH FLAT-LEAF PARSLEY

¼ CUP OLIVE OR SUNFLOWER OIL

1 TABLESPOON HARISSA (PAGE 48)

1 TEASPOON GROUND TURMERIC

1½ POUNDS VEAL SHANK OR BRISKET

2 POUNDS LAMB SHOULDER, BONED AND CUBED

4 FRESH ARTICHOKE HEARTS, DICED (PAGE 76)

2 POUNDS SPINACH OR YOUNG SWISS CHARD, STEMMED
    AND CUT INTO 1¼-INCH PIECES

1 *OSBANE* (PAGE 140; OPTIONAL)

⅓ CUP CHOPPED FRESH MINT

4 MATZOH

Cook the fava beans in boiling water for 2 minutes; drain. Pinch the beans from their skin. Set aside.

In a large bowl, combine the cardoons, carrots, cabbage, turnips, celery, celery root, and fennel. Add the ground rose petals, if using, the ground coriander, pepper, half the minced garlic, the onions, salt, and 3 tablespoons of the chopped fresh coriander. Add half of the dill and parsley. Mix well.

In a large soup pot, heat the oil over medium heat and stir in the harissa, the remaining garlic, and the turmeric. Add the meats and sauté for 5 minutes to coat with oil and spices. Add the mixed vegetables. Add water to cover and simmer 1 hour. Add the artichoke hearts, spinach or chard, favas, and *osbane,* if using. Cover and cook for 1 hour. Add the mint and the rest of the dill, fresh coriander, and parsley. Cook 15 minutes longer.

Break the matzoh into quarters and place on top of the vegetables. Serve hot or warm.

Note: Dried rose petals can be found in some spice and herb shops. They are also packaged as a tea. If you can't find them, you may leave them out.

: : : : : :

OSBANE

TUNISIAN SAUSAGE

Traditionally, this mixture is stuffed into beef intestines or stomach lining. You can wrap it in cheesecloth and tie it with string. *Osbane* is served in Algeria as well as Tunisia. Daisy Taieb omits tripe from her version. If you decide to omit the tripe, double the amount of ground beef.

Serves 6

7 OUNCES VEAL TRIPE, BLANCHED IN SALTED WATER AND CUT INTO SMALL CUBES, OR SUBSTITUTE AN ADDITIONAL $1/2$ POUND GROUND BEEF

$1/2$ POUND GROUND BEEF

2 ONIONS, CHOPPED

4 CLOVES GARLIC, MINCED

$1/4$ CUP CHOPPED FRESH CORIANDER (CILANTRO)

2 TABLESPOONS CHOPPED FRESH MINT

$1/2$ POUND CHOPPED SPINACH

2 TEASPOONS GROUND CORIANDER

1 EGG

$1/4$ CUP LONG-GRAIN RICE

2 TABLESPOONS OLIVE OIL

SALT AND FRESHLY GROUND BLACK PEPPER TO TASTE

1 TEASPOON HARISSA, OR TO TASTE (PAGE 48)

1 BAY LEAF

1 STALK OF CELERY

In a large bowl, combine all of the ingredients except for the bay leaf and celery stalk. Form into a sausage shape about 12 inches long and $3^{1}/2$ inches in diameter. Wrap in cheesecloth and tie both ends closed.

Add 5 to 6 inches salted water to a large pot. Add the bay leaf and celery. Bring to a boil, reduce heat to a simmer, and add the sausage. Cover and cook for 1 hour. Drain, let cool, and refrigerate for 1 to 2 hours.

Serve in slices, accompanied with braised lentils or a salad.

Variation: Tebaria A similar sausage is made with 2 diced carrots added to the meat mixture, which is then molded around a center of hard-cooked eggs.

: : : : : :

CHEMS *al* AACHI, *or* BOULETTES *de* VIANDE *et* SAUCE CRÉPUSCULE

MEATBALLS WITH SAFFRON SUNSET SAUCE

The Arab name of this dish, *chems el aachi,* means "setting sun" because the golden color of the sauce is reminiscent of a glorious sunset in Morocco. Vegetable-enriched meatballs are part the Sephardic culinary tradition of thrift. Here, grated potatoes help to stretch the amount of meat needed to make people feel satisfied. Interestingly enough, in John Cooper's *Eat and Be Satisfied* he refers to a recipe for *albondigas* in a saffron sauce from *Libro Novo,* published in Venice in 1549. Obviously, this was a dish of Arabic heritage that came with the Spanish Jews to Venice.

Serves 8

2 POUNDS GROUND BEEF

3 RUSSET POTATOES (ABOUT 1^1/$_2$ POUNDS), PEELED AND
  SHREDDED

2 EGGS, LIGHTLY BEATEN

^{1}/$_2$ CUP DRIED BREAD CRUMBS

^{1}/$_2$ TEASPOON GROUND MACE

SALT AND FRESHLY GROUND BLACK PEPPER TO TASTE

1 TEASPOON SAFFRON THREADS, CRUSHED AND
  INFUSED IN ^{1}/$_2$ CUP HOT WATER

^{1}/$_4$ CUP OLIVE OIL

3 CLOVES GARLIC, MINCED

1 BUNCH FRESH CORIANDER (CILANTRO), CHOPPED

1 TEASPOON SWEET PAPRIKA

1 TEASPOON GROUND TURMERIC

1 TEASPOON GROUND CUMIN

1 TEASPOON POWDERED CHICKEN STOCK, OR
  1 BOUILLON CUBE, CRUSHED, OR ^{1}/$_2$ CUP
  CHICKEN BROTH

^{1}/$_2$ CUP WATER

STEAMED RICE FOR SERVING

In a large bowl, combine the meat, shredded potatoes, and eggs. Add the bread crumbs, mace, salt, pepper, and ^{1}/$_4$ cup of the saffron infusion. Knead well with your hands to mix. Form into walnut-sized meatballs. Set aside.

In a large sauté pan or skillet, heat the oil and add the garlic, fresh coriander, spices, powdered chicken stock or bouillon cube, and 2 tablespoons of the saffron infusion. Cook until the sauce turns yellow, then add the water. Add the meatballs in one layer and simmer until cooked through, 25 to 30 minutes. Add the remaining saffron infusion and heat through. Taste and adjust the seasoning. Serve hot, with rice.

: : : : : :

COUSCOUS IMPERIAL

IMPERIAL COUSCOUS

This is my recipe for a basic couscous meal. It can
be made with beef, lamb, or chicken. This version
is a cross between one from Tangier and one from
Fez. Algerian cooks prefer beef or chicken for their
couscous, not lamb. Sometimes beef and chicken are
used together. Meatballs may replace the chunks of
meat or poultry (see page 152 for a basic meatball
recipe). On Rosh Hashanah, cooked quince may be
added along with raisins to add sweetness for the
new year. If served on the night before Passover,
fresh favas are added. If the stew is served with barley couscous, it's called *tchicha;* if served with new
wheat, the dish is called *azenbo.* In other words, the
stew remains constant, but if the grain changes, the
name changes, too.

Serves 6 TO 8

1 CUP DRIED CHICKPEAS, SOAKED IN COLD WATER
    OVERNIGHT
2 POUNDS STEWING BEEF OR LAMB CUT INTO 2-INCH
    PIECES, OR 1 CHICKEN, CUT INTO SERVING PORTIONS
2 LARGE ONIONS, CHOPPED
2 TEASPOONS SALT
2 TEASPOONS FRESHLY GROUND BLACK PEPPER
2 TEASPOONS GROUND GINGER
1/2 TEASPOON SAFFRON THREADS, CRUSHED AND
    STEEPED IN 1/4 CUP HOT WATER OR BROTH
1/4 CUP OLIVE OIL
WATER OR MEAT OR POULTRY BROTH AS NEEDED
6 LARGE OR 12 SMALL CARROTS, PEELED AND CUT
    INTO 11/2-INCH CHUNKS
3 LARGE OR 6 SMALL TURNIPS, PEELED AND QUARTERED
    OR CUT INTO 11/2-INCH PIECES
1 POUND PUMPKIN SQUASH, PEELED AND CUT INTO
    11/2- TO 2-INCH CHUNKS

3 TOMATOES, PEELED, SEEDED, AND CHOPPED
6 SMALL ZUCCHINI, CUT INTO 2-INCH LENGTHS
1/2 CUP GOLDEN RAISINS
4 COOKED QUINCE (PAGE 126; OPTIONAL)
1/2 CUP ALMONDS, TOASTED (OPTIONAL)
COUSCOUS FOR SERVING (PAGE 83)
HONEY TO TASTE (OPTIONAL)
HARISSA TO TASTE (PAGE 48)

Drain and rinse the chickpeas. Put in a soup pot and
cover with cold water. Bring to a boil, reduce heat
to a simmer, cover, and cook until tender, 45 to 60
minutes. Drain and let cool.

In a soup pot, combine the meat, onions, salt, pepper,
ginger, saffron infusion, and oil. Turn the meat and
vegetables in the oil to coat, then add water or broth
to cover. Bring to a boil, reduce heat to a simmer,
cover, and cook meat for 1 hour and chicken or meatballs for 30 minutes. Add the cooked chickpeas and
all the vegetables except the zucchini. Cook for 30
minutes, then add the zucchini, raisins, and the
quince and almonds, if using. Cover and cook until
all the vegetables and meats are tender.

Pile the couscous on a platter. Surround with meat
and vegetables, or make a well in the center and
put them in. Taste the pan juices and adjust the
seasoning. If you like, add a bit of honey. Reserve
1 cup of the juices and spoon the rest over the meat
and vegetables. Mix harissa with the reserved juices
and pass alongside.

: : : : : :

D'FINA DJERBALIYA

LAMB STEW FROM DJERBA

The Tunisian island of Djerba once was home to a sizeable Jewish community. This Sabbath *d'fina* is named for the island. You can make it with beef as well as lamb. This is an ideal dish for Rosh Hashanah as well as for the Sabbath.

Serves 6 TO 8

1/2 CUP DRIED CHICKPEAS, SOAKED OVERNIGHT IN
    2 CUPS WATER AND DRAINED

1/2 CUP DRIED APRICOTS, SOAKED IN HOT WATER FOR
    2 TO 3 HOURS

1/2 CUP PITTED PRUNES, SOAKED IN HOT WATER FOR
    2 TO 3 HOURS

1 CUP RAISINS SOAKED IN HOT WATER FOR 1 HOUR
    (OPTIONAL)

1/4 CUP OLIVE OIL

4 POUNDS LAMB SHOULDER, TRIMMED OF
    EXCESS FAT AND CUT INTO 2-INCH CUBES
    (3 POUNDS STEWING MEAT, AFTER TRIMMING)

2 TO 3 ONIONS, DICED (ABOUT 4 CUPS)

1 LARGE GREEN BELL PEPPER, SEEDED, DERIBBED,
    AND DICED

4 CLOVES GARLIC, MINCED

1/2 TEASPOON GROUND ALLSPICE OR CINNAMON

1 TEASPOON GROUND CUMIN

1/2 TEASPOON CAYENNE PEPPER

1 TEASPOON FRESHLY GROUND BLACK PEPPER

2 CUPS WATER OR MEAT BROTH

SALT TO TASTE

COUSCOUS FOR SERVING (PAGE 83)

Put the chickpeas in a medium saucepan and cover with cold water. Bring to a boil, reduce heat to a simmer, cover, and cook until tender, about 1 hour. Set aside.

Drain and coarsely chop the soaked fruit. Set aside.

In a large sauté pan or skillet, heat the oil over high heat and brown the cubed meat on all sides. Using a slotted spoon, transfer to a casserole.

Add the onions, bell pepper, and garlic to the pan and cook over medium heat for about 10 minutes. Add the spices and cook for 5 minutes. Add the vegetable mixture and the water or broth to the meat in the casserole. Cover and cook for about 1 hour. Add the chopped fruits and chickpeas. Cook until the meat and chickpeas are tender, about 30 minutes. Season with salt. Serve with couscous.

: : : : : :

MROUZIA

LAMB TAGINE WITH PRUNES AND HONEY

Called *lham lhalou* in Algeria, this dish is often
served on the second night of Rosh Hashanah, when
a sweet new year is celebrated with sweet food. It is
not served on the first night, as prunes are black
and no black food is permitted then. Simy Danan
adds a mixture of dried fruits such as apricots,
pears, and raisins. You could serve this on the first
night by just omitting prunes and using the apricots and raisins. One cup toasted blanched almonds
may be added instead of sesame seeds. You may also
make this with beef.

Serves 6 TO 8

3 TO 4 TABLESPOONS OLIVE OIL

4 POUNDS LAMB SHOULDER, CUT INTO $1^1/2$- TO
    2-INCH CUBES

3 YELLOW ONIONS, CHOPPED

$1^1/2$ TEASPOONS GROUND CINNAMON

1 TEASPOON GROUND GINGER

2 TEASPOONS GROUND CORIANDER

$1/4$ TEASPOON CRUSHED SAFFRON THREADS

$1/2$ TEASPOON FRESHLY GROUND BLACK PEPPER,
    PLUS MORE TO TASTE

2 TO 3 CUPS LAMB BROTH OR WATER, OR AS NEEDED

1 POUND PITTED PRUNES, SOAKED IN WATER
    FOR 1 HOUR

$1/3$ CUP DARK HONEY, OR TO TASTE

SALT TO TASTE

3 TABLESPOONS SESAME SEEDS, TOASTED

COUSCOUS FOR SERVING (PAGE 83)

In a large sauté pan or skillet, heat the oil over medium
heat and brown the lamb on all sides. Using a slotted
spoon, transfer to a casserole. Sauté the onions in the
same pan over medium heat until tender, about
8 minutes. Add the cinnamon, ginger, ground
coriander, saffron, and the $1/2$ teaspoon pepper and
cook for 3 minutes. Pour over the lamb, adding
enough broth or water to barely cover the meat and
onion mixture. Bring to a boil and reduce heat to
a simmer. Cover and cook for about 45 minutes.
Drain the prunes and add to the stew. Simmer until
the meat is tender, about 20 minutes. Add the honey,
salt, and pepper. Sprinkle with the sesame seeds.
Serve with couscous.

*Variation: Mrouzia (Lamb with Raisins, Almonds,
and Honey)* Replace the prunes with 2 cups plumped
raisins, and replace the sesame seeds with $1^1/2$ cups
blanched almonds. This is a Passover specialty of Fez
and Meknes.

Note: Chicken or squab may be used instead
of lamb in both recipes.

: : : : : :

MECHOUI

ROAST LAMB WITH MOROCCAN SPICES

The term *mechoui* refers to a whole lamb cooked on the spit. It is prepared on very special occasions, for big parties and during Passover, because supposedly it is what the Jews would have cooked in the wilderness during the exodus from Egypt. While a whole lamb is not a likely option for home cooks, for special occasions a leg of lamb would be the best cut for this recipe. However, most observant Jews do not cook the hindquarters of an animal, in memory of a passage in Genesis where Jacob battled with the angel, was injured, and became lame. It's not that leg of lamb is forbidden; it is just that before eating a hindquarter, the sciatic nerve and blood vessels attached to it must be removed, a time-consuming process. So I was surprised to find a recipe for leg of lamb in the book *Moroccan Jewish Cookery,* by Viviane and Nina Moryoussef. The most strictly observant Jews would use lamb shoulder. For a very festive meal, you may want to splurge and use racks of lamb, or if you are observant, have a butcher bone the leg of lamb and remove the vein. Leg of lamb cut into $1^{1}/_{2}$-inch cubes and threaded on skewers would be ideal.

This brings us to the next issue, the degree of doneness. Many of us have come to prefer rare to medium-rare for lamb chops and leg of lamb, for juiciness, texture, and flavor. In kosher cooking, all meat is cooked well done so there is no visible blood. The meat is first salted and soaked. This is fine for stews made with shoulder, and even for meatballs, but this treatment poses a dilemma for those who love lamb chops or leg of lamb cooked to a lesser degree of doneness. The timing is up to you. You may decide to stay with the spirit of the dish but not cook it in a kosher manner. *Mechoui* is accompanied with an assortment of salads. Lemon wedges and harissa thinned with oil and lemon juice are the traditional condiments.

Serves 6 TO 8

2 TEASPOONS GROUND CUMIN

$1^{1}/_{2}$ TEASPOONS GROUND CORIANDER

$^{1}/_{2}$ TEASPOON CAYENNE PEPPER

2 TEASPOONS SWEET PAPRIKA

2 TEASPOONS FRESHLY GROUND BLACK PEPPER

6 TABLESPOONS EXTRA-VIRGIN OLIVE OIL, PLUS MORE FOR RACKS OF LAMB, IF USING

$^{1}/_{4}$ CUP FRESH LEMON JUICE

2 TABLESPOONS MINCED GARLIC, PLUS 3 CLOVES GARLIC, CUT INTO SLIVERS

$^{1}/_{2}$ CUP CHOPPED FRESH CORIANDER (CILANTRO)

ONE 4- TO 5-POUND BONED LAMB SHOULDER, OR 3 RACKS OF LAMB, ENDS TRIMMED, OR ONE 6-POUND BONELESS LEG OF LAMB

COUSCOUS WITH ALMONDS AND RAISINS, FOR SERVING (PAGE 83)

LEMON WEDGES FOR SERVING

HARISSA (PAGE 48) FOR SERVING

In a small bowl, combine the spices, the 6 tablespoons olive oil, the lemon juice, minced garlic, and fresh coriander. Stir to make a paste.

If using racks of lamb, make incisions with a small sharp knife between the chops and insert the slivers of garlic. Rub the lamb with the paste and marinate at room temperature for 2 hours or in the refrigerator overnight. Preheat the oven to 450 degrees F. In a large ovenproof skillet, heat the oil over high heat and sear the racks on all sides. Roast until an instant-read thermometer inserted in the center and not touching bone registers 120 degrees F for rare, 130 degrees F for medium-rare, or 140 degrees F for medium, 12 to 20 minutes.

If using shoulder of lamb or leg of lamb, spread it with half of the paste, then roll it up and tie it closed.

Insert the garlic slivers in the folds and rub with the remaining paste. Marinate as above. Preheat the oven to 350 degrees F. Roast the shoulder for about $1^1/_2$ hours, or until an instant-read thermometer inserted in the center registers 160 degrees F for well done. For the leg of lamb, roast for about 1 hour, 10 minutes; the thermometer should register 120 degrees F for rare, 130 degrees F for medium. Let rest for 10 minutes before carving. The lamb will continue to cook as it rests.

You may also rub the paste on a butterflied leg of lamb and not roll it up. Marinate, then grill or broil for 8 to 10 minutes per side.

Serve with couscous with almonds and raisins. Pass lemon wedges and harissa at table.

Note: This spice paste would also work well on lamb kebabs. Thread the meat on skewers, alternating with thin slivers of onions. Rub with the paste and marinate as above. Broil or grill to the desired degree of doneness, turning once. Serve with bowls of ground toasted cumin mixed with salt for dipping.

: : : : : :

LOUBIA, *or* LUBIYA M'SALLAT

WHITE BEAN AND MEAT STEW

Jacqueline Cohen-Azuelos's mother's recipe for *loubia* is related to the Spanish *cocido* and the French *cassoulet,* as it has meat and sausage mixed with the beans. This classic Sabbath dish is a *d'fina* and is prepared before sundown the night before it is to be served. An Algerian version uses veal shanks and 1 whole head of garlic, sometimes with tomatoes, sometimes not, and sweet paprika. The Syrian and Egyptian versions of this bean and meat stew is called *lubiya,* and may use black-eyed peas or white beans. Veal is traditionally used instead of beef, and no sausage or shank bones are added. In the Algerian city of Constantine, they add a meat loaf called *coclo,* much as in the Moroccan *skhina* on page 136.

Serves 8

2 TABLESPOONS OLIVE OIL

2 TABLESPOONS PEANUT OIL

6 TO 8 CLOVES GARLIC, SMASHED

2 TOMATOES, CHOPPED

2 TABLESPOONS CHOPPED FRESH FLAT-LEAF PARSLEY

2 POUNDS DRIED WHITE BEANS, SOAKED OVERNIGHT AND DRAINED

5 VEAL SHANKS

2 1/2 POUNDS STEWING BEEF

1 ALGERIAN COCLO (RECIPE FOLLOWS; OPTIONAL)

SALT AND FRESHLY GROUND BLACK PEPPER TO TASTE

1 CUP TOMATO PUREE

GRATED ZEST OF 1 ORANGE

1 TEASPOON GROUND CUMIN

SMOKED BEEF SAUSAGES, SLICED (OPTIONAL)

In a large soup pot, heat the oils over medium heat and sauté the garlic for 2 to 3 minutes. Add the chopped tomatoes and parsley and mix well. Add the beans, then arrange the veal shanks and chunks of beef on top, and *coclo,* if using. Sprinkle with salt and pepper and cover with water. Bring to a boil. Reduce heat to low, cover, and cook for 1 1/2 hours. Add the tomato puree, orange zest, and cumin. Cover and cook until all the fat rises to the surface, about 30 minutes. Refrigerate overnight. Remove the congealed fat. Reheat, adding the sausages, if using, stirring often to prevent sticking. Ladle into shallow soup bowls.

ALGERIAN COCLO (MEAT LOAF)

2 POUNDS GROUND BEEF

8 CLOVES GARLIC, MINCED

2 TABLESPOONS CHOPPED FRESH CORIANDER (CILANTRO)

1 TEASPOON CARAWAY SEEDS

3 SLICES BREAD, SOAKED IN WATER AND SQUEEZED DRY

3 TO 4 EGGS

SALT AND FRESHLY GROUND BLACK PEPPER TO TASTE

In a large bowl, combine all the ingredients and mix well. Form into a loaf 10 to 12 inches long and 4 to 5 inches wide (form it to fit the pan). Wrap the loaf in cheesecloth and tie at both ends. Poach this atop the bean stew. Let cool a bit before slicing. Some squeeze lemon juice on at the table.

: : : : : :

MERGUEZ

SPICY ALGERIAN SAUSAGES

The meat for *merguez* should not be too lean. It needs fat if it is to remain juicy. *Merguez* is usually broiled or grilled. Tunisians add the minced cloves of almost a head of garlic and use fewer spices. Lamb casing may be ordered from your butcher. Wash well and run water through the casings. If not using casing, form into patties.

Makes 12 TO 18 *merguez*

2½ POUNDS GROUND LAMB, BEEF, OR A MIXTURE

3 CLOVES GARLIC, MINCED

1 TABLESPOON GROUND CORIANDER (CILANTRO)

1 TABLESPOON GROUND CUMIN

2 TEASPOONS GROUND CARAWAY (OPTIONAL)

1 TABLESPOON FRESHLY GROUND BLACK PEPPER

1 TABLESPOON SWEET PAPRIKA

2 TEASPOONS CAYENNE PEPPER OR TO TASTE

2 TEASPOONS SALT

¼ CUP OLIVE OIL

LAMB CASINGS, WELL RINSED (OPTIONAL)

Light a fire in a charcoal grill. (You may also use an oiled grill pan heated over medium-high heat.)

In a large bowl, combine all the ingredients except the casings. Stuff into casings, if using, and tie off into 3-inch lengths. Prick with a fork to release the fat. Or, form the mixture into patties. Grill until cooked through but juicy.

: : : : : :

RAGOUT *d'*ARTICHAUTS FARCIS

STUFFED ARTICHOKE STEW

Braised artichokes stuffed with meat are popular throughout the Middle East and North Africa. Leone Jaffin's Algerian recipe adds peas and pearl onions for a very pretty presentation. Some cooks use mashed potato instead of rice for binding the meat filling. Others add a bit of ground cumin. Stuffed artichoke hearts are called *kharshouf mahshi* in Egypt, where they are filled with meat, onions, and pine nuts but no rice or bread.

Serves 8

For the meatballs:

14 OUNCES GROUND BEEF

2 TABLESPOONS RAW RICE

3 CLOVES GARLIC, MINCED

3 TABLESPOONS CHOPPED FRESH FLAT-LEAF PARSLEY

1 TEASPOON GROUND ALLSPICE IN ARABIC VERSION
    (OPTIONAL)

1 TEASPOON GROUND CUMIN IN MOROCCAN VERSION
    (OPTIONAL)

1 EGG, BEATEN

1 TABLESPOON PEANUT OIL

8 FRESH ARTICHOKE HEARTS (PAGE 76)

3 TABLESPOONS PEANUT OIL

12 PEARL ONIONS

1½ CUPS WATER

PINCH OF CRUSHED SAFFRON THREADS

1 BAY LEAF

SALT TO TASTE

2½ POUNDS (ABOUT 2½ CUPS) GREEN PEAS, SHELLED
    (OPTIONAL)

PINCH OF SUGAR (OPTIONAL)

COOKED FRESH NOODLES OR SAFFRON RICE PILAF
    FOR SERVING

To make the meatballs, in a medium bowl, combine all the ingredients and mix well. Form into 8 meatballs. Drain the artichoke hearts and stuff 1 meatball into each.

In a large sauté pan or skillet, heat the oil over medium-high heat. Sauté the onions until they take on a bit of color, about 5 minutes. Add the water, saffron, bay leaf, and salt. Bring to a boil, add the artichoke hearts, and reduce heat to a simmer. Cover and cook for 20 to 30 minutes, then add the peas and sugar, if using. Cook until peas and artichokes are tender, about 5 to 10 minutes.

Serve with noodles or pilaf. During Passover, this stew is served with potatoes.

TUNISIAN VARIATION (FROM DAISY TAIEB)
For the stuffing:
$3/4$ POUND GROUND BEEF
4 INCHES STALE BREAD, SOAKED IN WATER AND
   SQUEEZED DRY
2 TABLESPOONS CHOPPED FRESH FLAT-LEAF PARSLEY
3 CLOVES GARLIC, MINCED
2 TABLESPOONS CHOPPED FRESH MINT, OR
   1 TABLESPOON DRIED MINT
SALT AND FRESHLY GROUND BLACK PEPPER TO TASTE
FRESHLY GRATED NUTMEG TO TASTE
2 HARD-COOKED EGGS, CHOPPED

4 LARGE NEW POTATOES
12 FRESH ARTICHOKE HEARTS (PAGE 76)

For the sauce:
$1/4$ CUP OLIVE OIL
3 LARGE TOMATOES, PEELED, SEEDED, AND DICED
PINCH OF GROUND TURMERIC
1 BAY LEAF
PEEL OF $1/2$ PRESERVED LEMON, MINCED

To make the stuffing, in a medium bowl, combine all the ingredients and knead to mix well. Cut the potatoes in half and scoop out the centers with a melon baller to make a pocket for the stuffing. Stuff the filling into the artichoke hearts and potatoes.

To make the sauce, in a large sauté pan, or skillet, combine all the ingredients. Bring to a boil, reduce heat to a simmer, and cook for 5 minutes to reduce slightly. Add the stuffed vegetables in one layer. Add enough water to just cover the vegetables without dislodging the meatball filling. Bring to a boil, reduce heat to a simmer, cover, and cook until the vegetables are tender, about 30 minutes.

: : : : : :

PETITS OISEAUX *aux* CARDES

LITTLE BIRDS WITH CARDOONS

These are not really birds, but meatballs stuffed between two pieces of cardoon, then braised and sauced in the Sephardic manner with an egg and lemon mixture. This Algerian recipe is from Leone Jaffin's *150 recettes et mille et un souvenirs d'une juive d'Algérie.* You could serve this for Passover if you used matzoh to hold the meatballs together instead of bread.

Serves 6

JUICE OF 1 LEMON
2 POUNDS CARDOONS

For the meatballs:
$3/4$ POUND GROUND BEEF
$1/2$ ONION, FINELY CHOPPED
1 SLICE BREAD, SOAKED IN WATER AND SQUEEZED DRY
1 TABLESPOON CHOPPED FRESH FLAT-LEAF PARSLEY
1 EGG, BEATEN
$1/2$ TEASPOON GROUND CUMIN OR CARAWAY
SALT AND FRESHLY GROUND BLACK PEPPER TO TASTE
CHOPPED FRESH MINT TO TASTE (OPTIONAL)

For the sauce:
3 TABLESPOONS PEANUT OIL
$1/4$ TEASPOON SAFFRON THREADS, CRUSHED
1 BAY LEAF
$1 1/2$ CUPS WATER
SALT AND FRESHLY GROUND BLACK PEPPER TO TASTE
2 EGG YOLKS
JUICE OF 1 LEMON

BOILED POTATOES FOR SERVING

Fill a large bowl with water and add the lemon juice. Trim the prickly leaves from the cardoons and pull off the strings. Cut into 3-inch pieces and drop into the lemon water until ready to cook. Drain the cardoons and put in a large saucepan of salted water. Bring to a boil and cook for about 10 minutes. Drain well and set aside.

To make the meatballs, in a medium bowl, combine all the ingredients. Knead well to mix. Form into ovals about 2 inches long and 1 inch in diameter. Stuff a meatball between 2 pieces of cardoon. Tie closed with kitchen string.

To make the sauce, in a large sauté pan or skillet, heat the oil over medium heat and add the saffron, bay leaf, water, salt, and pepper. Bring to a boil. Add the "birds" and cook until most of the liquid has been absorbed and the cardoons are tender, about 30 minutes. Using a slotted spoon, transfer the birds to a platter.

Beat the egg yolks with the lemon juice. Whisk this mixture into the pan juices and remove from heat. Spoon the sauce over the birds. Serve with boiled potatoes.

: : : : : :

KRA'A

LEBANESE STUFFED SQUASH WITH APRICOT SAUCE

This would be an ideal dish for the Rosh Hashanah table. The sweetness of the new year is echoed in the sweetness of the apricots. There are three ways to stuff the zucchini. To do it the hard way, hollow them out with an apple corer and keep them whole. Or, you can cut them in half lengthwise and scoop out the seeds, forming barquettes. A Moroccan method is to first peel the zucchini in a striped fashion. Cut off the ends, then cut the zucchini into $1\frac{1}{2}$- to 2-inch pieces. Scoop out the pulp, leaving a shell about $\frac{1}{3}$ inch thick. The tart-sweet tamarind paste, or *temerhendy,* is found in stores that specialize in Middle Eastern foods.

Serves 6

12 ZUCCHINI

For the stuffing:
1 POUND GROUND BEEF
$\frac{1}{2}$ CUP BASMATI RICE, SOAKED IN COLD WATER FOR
    30 MINUTES
$\frac{1}{2}$ TEASPOON GROUND CINNAMON
$\frac{1}{2}$ TEASPOON GROUND ALLSPICE
1 TEASPOON SALT
2 TABLESPOONS WATER

$2\frac{1}{2}$ CUPS WATER
$\frac{1}{2}$ TEASPOON SALT

1 CUP DRIED APRICOTS, SOAKED IN HOT WATER FOR
    30 MINUTES
$\frac{1}{4}$ CUP FRESH LEMON JUICE
2 TABLESPOONS SUGAR
2 TABLESPOONS TAMARIND PASTE, DISSOLVED IN $\frac{1}{4}$ CUP
    WATER, OR 2 TABLESPOONS POMEGRANATE MOLASSES

Cut the zucchini in half lengthwise and scoop out the pulp with small melon baller. Chop and reserve the pulp.

To make the stuffing, in a medium bowl, combine all the ingredients along with the chopped pulp and knead to mix well. Stuff this into the zucchini. Any leftover meat mixture can be formed into meatballs.

Arrange the stuffed zucchini in a large sauté pan or skillet. Add the water and salt. Arrange any extra meatballs among the zucchini. Bring to a simmer, cover, and cook for 10 minutes. Set aside.

In a small saucepan, combine the apricots and their soaking water, lemon juice, sugar, and tamarind mixture or pomegranate molasses. Simmer for 10 minutes, then add to the zucchini. Cover and cook over low heat until the squash is tender and the apricots have formed a sauce, about 35 minutes. Check from time to time to make sure there is enough liquid in the pan to prevent scorching.

Variation: Les Courgettes Farci (Moroccan Meat-Stuffed Zucchini) Simmer the meatball-filled zucchini in an onion and tomato sauce seasoned with cinnamon and saffron.

: : : : : :

KEFTA *de* VIANDE *au* CUMIN
et CONFITURE *d'*OIGNON *et*
SAUCE *aux* TOMATES

CUMIN-FLAVORED MEATBALLS WITH ONION JAM AND SPICY TOMATO SAUCE

Helene Ganz Perez in *Marrakech la rouge* serves meatballs with onion confiture. In *Saveurs de mon enfance,* a few mint leaves are added to the meat mixture, and a bit less cumin. Meatballs are sometimes called *boundigas,* echoing the Spanish word *albondigas. Kefta* can be round or flat in shape. Although there is a temptation to treat them as burgers and serve them rare, in the kosher kitchen these are well cooked. Moroccan *kefta* that are to be grilled do not have bread crumbs as a binder; only those sautéed as meatballs, or *boulettes,* will have such an addition.

Serves 4

1 POUND GROUND BEEF

2 TO 3 TABLESPOONS OLIVE OIL

3 CLOVES GARLIC, MINCED

2 TABLESPOONS CHOPPED FRESH FLAT-LEAF PARSLEY

2 TABLESPOONS CHOPPED FRESH CORIANDER (CILANTRO)

1 TABLESPOON GROUND CUMIN

$^1/_4$ TEASPOON CAYENNE PEPPER

$1^1/_2$ TEASPOONS SALT

$^1/_2$ TEASPOON FRESHLY GROUND BLACK PEPPER

CONFITURE D'OIGNONS (PAGE 156)

SAUCE AUX TOMATES (PAGE 156)

Light a fire in a charcoal grill. (You may also use a skillet heated over medium-high heat.)

In a medium bowl, combine all the ingredients except the jam and sauce. Mix well. Form into 16 oval meatballs wrapped around skewers, or into 8 oval patties. Grill or cook in oil on a hot pan until browned on all sides. Serve with onion jam and tomato sauce.

Moroccan Variation: Combine 1 pound ground beef with 1 bunch chopped stemmed fresh coriander (cilantro), 3 chopped fresh mint leaves, 1 teaspoon *each* ground cumin and sweet paprika, $1^1/_2$ teaspoons salt, and $^1/_2$ teaspoon freshly ground black pepper. Knead well, form into balls, and flatten. Grill or fry until golden brown. Serve with harissa (page 48).

Syrian Variation: Combine 1 pound ground beef, $^1/_2$ cup finely chopped onion, 6 tablespoons minced fresh flat-leaf parsley, 4 eggs, $^1/_4$ cup dry bread crumbs, $1^1/_2$ teaspoons salt, 1 teaspoon ground allspice, $^1/_2$ teaspoon ground cinnamon, and $^1/_2$ teaspoon freshly ground black pepper. Form into small patties, fry, and serve with pita bread and spicy tomato sauce (page 156).

CONFITURE D'OIGNONS|ONION JAM

Some onion jams are seasoned with a mixture of sweet spices such as ginger, mace, nutmeg, cinnamon, and cloves, or ras al hanout but this simpler version is seasoned only with cinnamon and sugar.

Makes 2$\frac{1}{2}$ TO 3 *cups*

3 TABLESPOONS OLIVE OIL

3 POUNDS ONIONS, CUT INTO HALF-ROUND SLICES
    OR CHOPPED

1 TABLESPOON GROUND CINNAMON, OR
    2 TABLESPOONS RAS AL HANOUT (PAGE 49)

$\frac{1}{4}$ CUP SUGAR OR HONEY

1 TEASPOON SALT

In a large sauté pan or skillet, heat the oil over medium heat. Add the onions and cook, stirring often, until very soft and golden, about 15 minutes. Add the remaining ingredients, reduce heat to low, and cook and stir until the onions are dark brown, aromatic, and the consistency of jam, 35 to 45 minutes. Serve warm. Keeps in the refrigerator for about 1 week.

SAUCE AUX TOMATES|SPICY TOMATO SAUCE

Makes about 1$\frac{3}{4}$ *cups*

$\frac{1}{4}$ CUP RAISINS, PLUMPED IN HOT WATER TO COVER
    FOR 15 MINUTES, NOT DRAINED

1$\frac{1}{2}$ CUPS TOMATO PUREE

1 TO 2 CLOVES GARLIC

1 TABLESPOON OLIVE OIL

1 TABLESPOON FRESH LEMON JUICE

$\frac{1}{2}$ TEASPOON CAYENNE PEPPER

PINCH OF GROUND CINNAMON

In a blender or food processor, combine all the ingredients and puree. Transfer to a small saucepan and simmer for 20 minutes until thickened. Serve warm or at room temperature. Store, covered in the refrigerator for up to 5 days.

: : : : : :

KIBBEH *bil* SINAYEH

BAKED LAYERED BULGUR AND MEAT

Traditionally, *kibbeh* are little football-shaped rounds of bulgur wheat mixed with meat and stuffed with a meat mixture. They are time-consuming to prepare and practice is required to make them right. This is a simpler but equally traditional way to make *kibbeh: bil sinayeh,* or "on a tray."

Serves 6 TO 8

For the stuffing:

3 TABLESPOONS OLIVE OIL

2 ONIONS, FINELY CHOPPED

1 1/2 POUNDS LEAN GROUND BEEF OR LAMB

SALT TO TASTE

1 TEASPOON FRESHLY GROUND BLACK PEPPER

1/4 CUP PINE NUTS, LIGHTLY TOASTED

For the kibbeh mixture:

2 CUPS BULGUR WHEAT OR FINE CRACKED WHEAT

1 POUND LEAN GROUND BEEF OR LAMB

2 ONIONS, FINELY CHOPPED

1 TABLESPOON GROUND CUMIN

2 TEASPOONS SALT

1 TEASPOON FRESHLY GROUND BLACK PEPPER

PINCH OF CAYENNE PEPPER

1/3 TO 1/2 CUP COLD WATER

1/2 CUP (1 STICK) MARGARINE, MELTED

To make the stuffing: In a large sauté pan, or skillet, heat the oil over medium heat and cook the onions for 8 minutes. Add the beef or lamb and cook until browned, stirring to break up any clumps. Add the salt, pepper, and pine nuts. Set aside.

To make the *kibbeh,* soak the bulgur or cracked wheat in cold salted water for 10 to 15 minutes. Drain and mix with the meat, onions, cumin, salt, pepper, and cayenne. Knead well by hand or in a food processor to make a paste. Add the water gradually while kneading.

Preheat the oven to 350 degrees F. Grease a 9-by-12-inch baking dish with margarine or oil. Put half the kibbeh mixture in the pan and pat it down evenly. Add the stuffing in an even layer, then top with the remaining *kibbeh* mixture. Smooth the top layer, then score it with a knife into diamond shapes as if cutting for baklava, and loosen the edges away from the side of the pan. Pour the margarine over the top and bake until top is golden and crunchy, about 45 minutes. You may also choose to brown the top under the broiler for added color and crunch. Serve hot.

: : : : : :

chapter 8

✹

SWEETS

In most Mediterranean countries, dessert is not an everyday affair. After the meal, fresh or dried fruit is offered. Occasionally, a rice or apricot pudding may be served. Most pastries are served on special occasions, on holidays such as Mimouna, on special tea or coffee afternoons, and at festive breakfast parties.

The Sephardic kitchen prides itself on its preserves and jams, so you will find recipes here for orange, quince, and eggplant conserves, as well as a raisin and walnut preserve that can be used as a filling for a tart.

There are very few large pastries in this part of the world. A ceremonial cake called *le paille* (from the English word *pie*) is based on the classic Spanish *panaspana,* or sponge cake. It can be served unadorned or layered with fruits, jam, almond paste, chocolate, or a meringue icing. Small pastries are the norm. They are literally finger foods, as they are eaten with the hands. Cookies, sweet *briouats,* and fruit-and-nut confections are most common. These are rather intense little morsels. After a full meal, one of these small sweet bites will sate your desire for a happy finale.

HAROSET

PASSOVER FRUIT CONDIMENT

Haroset is an essential part of the Passover Seder. This sweet fruit condiment represents the mortar that held the stones of the pyramids together. Most *harosets* are a paste that combines finely chopped dried fruits, nuts, wine, and occasionally fresh fruits like apples, pears, or bananas. *Haroset* may be cooked or uncooked. Often, North African *haroset* is rolled into little balls rather than served as a spread. The Moryoussef family used to wrap *haroset* balls in rose petals.

Makes $3^1/2$ TO 4 *cups*

ALGERIAN HAROSET:

$1^3/4$ CUPS CHOPPED PITTED DATES

$1^3/4$ CUPS CHOPPED DRIED FIGS

$1/4$ CUP DRY OR SWEET RED WINE

1 TEASPOON GROUND CINNAMON

$1/4$ TEASPOON FRESHLY GRATED NUTMEG

2 TABLESPOONS CONFECTIONERS' SUGAR

In a food processor, combine all the ingredients and pulse to a paste. Roll into walnut-sized balls.

Variation: Add 1 cup almonds and $1/2$ cup raisins to the paste.

MOROCCAN HAROSET FROM MARRAKECH:

1 POUND DATES, PITTED

2 CUPS WALNUTS, CHOPPED

$1/2$ CUP SWEET WINE

In a food processor, combine all the ingredients and pulse to a paste. Roll into 1-inch balls.

MOROCCAN COOKED HAROSET FROM TETOUAN:

Makes 5 TO 6 *cups*

1 PEAR, PEELED, CORED, AND DICED

3 APPLES, PEELED, CORED, AND CHOPPED

3 BANANAS, PEELED AND MASHED

1 POUND DATES, PITTED

$1/2$ POUND BLANCHED ALMONDS

2 TABLESPOONS GROUND CINNAMON

1 CUP SWEET WINE

In a food processor, combine all the ingredients and puree. Transfer the mixture to a saucepan and simmer over low heat for 15 to 20 minutes, adding wine or water as needed. Let cool. Cover and refrigerate for 1 to 2 hours to chill. Serve as a spread.

: : : : : :

CONFITURE *des* COINGS

QUINCE CONSERVE

In Algeria, a bowl of stewed quince or quince conserve is a traditional finale after the Rosh Hashanah repast. Quince can be baked, cooked in syrup, or turned into a fragrant terra-cotta-hued jam or paste. Quince paste is called *marmelo* in Portugal (the origin of the word *marmalade*) and *membrillo* in Spain. You can buy them, but you might want to make your own.

Makes about 4 half-pints

2 POUNDS QUINCE

3 TO 3 1/2 CUPS SUGAR

1 TEASPOON GROUND CINNAMON (OPTIONAL)

Wipe the fuzz off the quince and wash them well. Peel the quince, cut them into quarters, and remove the cores and seeds. Reserve the peels, cores, and seeds and tie them in a cheesecloth square. Slice the quince, place in a heavy enamel-lined Dutch oven, and add water to cover. Add the cheesecloth package. Bring to a boil, reduce heat to a low simmer, and cook until red and very tender, up to 1 hour. You may want to stop the cooking a few times, for about an hour or two, to let the quince rest and redden, then continue simmering. Add more water if needed.

(This process can take a day or two, if you like, and there is no need to refrigerate the quince in between simmerings.)

Remove and discard the cheesecloth bag. Drain and reserve any cooking liquid. Mash or puree the quince.

Measure the quince pulp together with any reserved liquid. Return to the pan. Add water to make 3 cups quince mixture. Add the sugar and cinnamon, if using. Cook over very low heat until very thick, about 30 minutes. Seal the quince jam in hot, sterilized jars and refrigerate for up to 1 month, or process for 10 minutes in a boiling-water bath and store in a cool pantry for several months.

Variation: To make a quince paste like Leone Jaffin's Aunt Germaine's, spread the quince puree on a marble slab or line a shallow baking pan with plastic wrap or parchment paper and spread out the puree to a thickness of 1/2 to 3/4 inch. Let dry for a few days in a warm place. Turn out onto a clean surface and cut into squares or lozenges. Roll in sugar and pack in an airtight container. If the quince paste is not firm enough to cut, roll it into balls and top with an almond or walnut. Serve as a candy.

: : : : : :

AUBERGINES CONFIT

CANDIED EGGPLANT

An eggplant conserve probably seems a bit strange to those of us with a Western mind set. Moussaka, yes. *Alla parmigiana,* yes. But sweets? While we don't think of eggplants as candidates for jam, they are a fruit, and preserving them in a rich sugar syrup has a long tradition in the Sephardic kitchen. To break the fast after Yom Kippur, Moroccan Jews in Essaouira serve *baraniya,* golden slices of fried eggplant dressed with sugar or half sugar and half honey, generously topped with toasted sesame seeds and cinnamon (see variation).

Makes about 4 pints

2 POUNDS JAPANESE OR BABY EGGPLANTS

2 CUPS WATER

4 CUPS SUGAR

2 CINNAMON STICKS

12 WHOLE CLOVES

1 TABLESPOON GROUND GINGER, OR 3 TABLESPOONS
    JULIENNED FRESH GINGER

1 CUP FRESH LEMON JUICE

Do not remove the stems of the eggplants. Prick the eggplants all over with a fork. Soak them in a bowl of cold water overnight. Drain. Bring a large pan of water to a boil and cook the eggplants for about 5 minutes. Drain again. Squeeze them lightly to rid them of excess water.

In a large saucepan, combine the 2 cups water, sugar, spices, and ginger. Simmer over low heat until as thick as honey, about 15 to 20 minutes. Add the lemon juice and eggplants and cook until most of the syrup is absorbed, about 1 hour, turning them occasionally. Discard the whole spices. With a slotted spoon, transfer the eggplants to 4 or 5 sterilized pint canning jars and seal. Process in a boiling-water bath for 10 minutes.

Variation: Gilda Angel's *baraniya* eggplant dish from Tangier is definitely Hispano-Arabic in origin. The honey is a giveaway. The eggplants are fried and chopped, seasoned with $1/2$ cup honey and $1/2$ teaspoon ground ginger or cinnamon, and cooked down to a jamlike consistency. One-half cup chopped toasted almonds are folded in, and sesame seeds are sprinkled over just before serving. This is spread on bread both before and after the Yom Kippur fast.

: : : : : :

ORANGES CONFIT

CANDIED ORANGES

This recipe is from Helene Ganz Perez's *Marrakech la rouge: les juifs de la medina.*

Makes 4 TO 5 pints

4 POUNDS VALENCIA ORANGES, SCRUBBED
JUICE OF 1 OR 2 LEMONS
8 CUPS SUGAR

Lightly scratch the outside of the oranges with a grater. Put the oranges into a large saucepan and cover with water. Bring to a low boil and cook until tender, 30 to 45 minutes. Drain and reserve the cooking liquid. Let the oranges cool to the touch, then cut them into quarters. Return the reserved cooking liquid to the pan, add the lemon juice and sugar, and stir over medium heat until sugar dissolves. Return the oranges to this syrup and bring to a rolling boil. Skim the foam, reduce heat to a simmer, and cook uncovered until the syrup thickens to the soft ball stage, 220 degrees F, about $1^{1}/_{2}$ hours. The oranges will have absorbed lots of syrup, the centers will be soft, and the skins will be translucent but firm.

With a slotted spoon, transfer the oranges to hot, sterilized jars and add syrup to cover. Seal and process in a boiling-water bath for 10 minutes.

Note: You could make this with tangerines.

: : : : : :

DATTES *à la* PÂTÉ *d'*AMANDES

DATES STUFFED WITH ALMOND PASTE

Stuffed dates are served at the end of the meal along with a platter of fresh fruit. Prunes may be stuffed the same way. Sometimes a bit of red food coloring is added to the almond paste to make it pink. If that is not festive enough, the dates may be dipped in colored sugar crystals.

Makes 2 dozen stuffed dates

For the filling:
2 CUPS (11 OUNCES) BLANCHED ALMONDS
$^{2}/_{3}$ CUP CONFECTIONERS' SUGAR
2 TABLESPOONS RUM, GRAND MARNIER, OR ORANGE-
    FLOWER WATER
1 TEASPOON ALMOND EXTRACT

24 LARGE MEDJOOL DATES, PARTIALLY SLICED OPEN
    AND PITTED
COLORED SUGAR FOR COATING (OPTIONAL)

To make the filling, in a food processor, grind the almonds with the sugar. Add the flavorings and process until the mixture comes together. Turn out onto a work surface and knead until smooth. Break off pieces and roll into oval balls. Stuff the paste into the dates. Roll the stuffed dates in the sugar, if using.

Note: You may also use commercial almond paste, softened by kneading in a mixer or by hand, to fill the dates.

: : : : : :

TARTE *au* CONFITURE *des* RAISINS *et* NOIX

RAISIN AND WALNUT JAM TART

Rich, rich, rich.

Serves 8

For the pastry dough:
2 CUPS ALL-PURPOSE FLOUR
$1/4$ CUP SUGAR
$1/2$ TEASPOON BAKING POWDER (OPTIONAL FOR A MORE
    TENDER CRUST)
$1/2$ CUP CANOLA OIL, OR $1/2$ CUP (1 STICK) COLD
    UNSALTED BUTTER, CUT TO BITS
1 EGG YOLK
1 TEASPOON VANILLA EXTRACT

$1/2$ RECIPE FOR MROZILLA (RECIPE FOLLOWS)

To make the dough by hand: In a medium bowl, combine the flour, sugar, and baking powder, if using. Add the oil or butter, egg yolk, and vanilla and stir to make a soft dough. To make the dough in a food processor: Combine the flour, sugar, and baking powder, if using, in a food processor. Pulse in the oil or butter, egg yolk, and vanilla until the dough just comes together. If using butter, wrap in plastic and refrigerate for 30 minutes.

Preheat the oven to 375 degrees F. Roll the dough out into a 12-inch circle between sheets of parchment paper and press the dough into an 8- or 9-inch tart pan with a removable bottom. Fill with the *mrozilla* and bake until the crust is golden and the top is set, 18 to 25 minutes.

Note: To top the tart with a lattice topping, increase the flour to $2^{1}/2$ cups, the butter to $3/4$ cup ($1^{1}/2$ sticks), and add a few tablespoons of ice water to hold the dough together.

: : : : : :

MROZILLA, *or* CONFITURE *des* RAISINS *et* NOIX

RAISIN AND WALNUT CONSERVE

This classic raisin and walnut conserve is often used as a filling for a dessert tart. This recipe was inspired by one in *Saveurs de mon enfance*.

Makes 8 TO 9 cups (enough filling for two 8-inch tarts)

2 CUPS SUGAR
3 CUPS WATER
1 CINNAMON STICK
5 WHOLE CLOVES
1 VANILLA BEAN, HALVED LENGTHWISE
$1^{1}/2$ POUNDS LARGE BLACK RAISINS, RINSED
    AND SEPARATED
$2^{1}/2$ CUPS WALNUTS

In a large saucepan, combine the sugar, water, cinnamon stick, cloves, and vanilla bean. (Some cooks add a bit of ground ginger or grated nutmeg.) Add the raisins and cook for 10 to 15 minutes over low heat. Add the nuts and simmer until slightly caramelized, about 10 minutes. Do not let this get too thick or it will set up like glue. Let cool, cover, and refrigerate for up to 1 month.

: : : : : :

ROZ *bil* HALEEB

SYRIAN RICE PUDDING

In early times, milk was so rare the Sephardim mixed ground almonds with boiling water to make almond milk as a substitute. Today, everyone has milk, and rice pudding is a beloved family dessert. *Roz bil haleeb* is served at dairy meals.

Serves 8

4 CUPS MILK

$2/3$ CUP SUGAR

ONE 3-INCH-LONG STRIP LEMON ZEST

1 CINNAMON STICK

3 CUPS WATER

PINCH OF SALT

$3/4$ CUP SHORT-GRAIN RICE

2 TABLESPOONS ROSE WATER OR ORANGE-FLOWER WATER, OR 1 TEASPOON VANILLA EXTRACT

CINNAMON FOR SPRINKLING

2 TABLESPOONS ALMONDS, CHOPPED, FOR GARNISH

In a large saucepan, combine the milk, sugar, lemon zest, and cinnamon stick. Bring to a boil. Remove from heat and set aside to steep for 30 minutes.

In a medium saucepan, bring the water to a boil, add the salt and rice, reduce heat to a simmer, and cook until the rice has swelled, 10 to 15 minutes. Drain. Add the rice to the milk and simmer slowly, stirring often, until thickened, 30 minutes or more. Discard the lemon zest and cinnamon stick.

Remove from heat and add the rose water, orange-flower water, or vanilla. Spoon the pudding into custard cups or a serving bowl. Sprinkle with cinnamon and garnish with chopped almonds.

: : : : : :

CRÈME *d'*AMARDINE

APRICOT PUDDING

This Lebanese pudding was traditionally prepared with sheets of dried apricot (*amardine,* or apricot leather), but it can also be made with dried apricots, which are more consistent in quality. Dried apricots may be sweet or quite tart, so you will have to adjust the sugar to suit your taste.

Serves 6 TO 8

3 CUPS (1 POUND) DRIED APRICOTS

4 CUPS WATER

$1/2$ CUP SUGAR, OR TO TASTE

2 TABLESPOONS CORNSTARCH DISSOLVED IN $1/4$ CUP WATER

1 TABLESPOON ORANGE-FLOWER WATER

FRESH LEMON JUICE TO TASTE

1 CUP HEAVY CREAM BEATEN WITH 2 TABLESPOONS SUGAR

2 TABLESPOONS PISTACHIO NUTS, TOASTED AND CHOPPED

Soak the apricots in the water overnight. In a large saucepan, cook the apricots and water until very soft, about 30 minutes, adding more water if needed. In a blender or food processor, puree the mixture. Return the puree to the pan and bring to a simmer. Stir in the sugar and cornstarch mixture. Simmer, stirring occasionally, until thickened, about 3 minutes. Stir in the orange-flower water and lemon juice. Transfer to 6 individual serving bowls. Refrigerate.

For a dairy meal, at serving time beat the cream with the sugar. Place a dollop of cream on each pudding and top with the chopped pistachio nuts.

: : : : : :

CRÈME *d'*AMARDINE ★ **APRICOT PUDDING**

MENENAS, *or* MAAMOUL

STUFFED BUTTER COOKIES

Called *menenas* by Sephardic Jews, these cookies, also known as *maamoul,* are very popular around Easter-time with non-Jews in Syria. Once you understand how to fold the dough around the filling, the cookies are easy to prepare. They can also be stuffed with nuts and dried fruits.

Makes about 30 *cookies*

For the nut filling:

2 CUPS ($^1/_2$ POUND) WALNUTS, ALMONDS, OR PISTACHIOS, FINELY CHOPPED

1 CUP SUGAR, OR TO TASTE

1 TABLESPOON ROSE WATER

2 TEASPOONS GROUND CINNAMON

1 CUP (2 STICKS) UNSALTED BUTTER AT ROOM TEMPERATURE

2 TABLESPOONS SUGAR

$3^1/_2$ CUPS SIFTED FLOUR

2 TO 4 TABLESPOONS MILK OR WATER

1 TABLESPOON ORANGE-FLOWER WATER OR ROSE WATER

CONFECTIONERS' SUGAR FOR DUSTING

To make the filling: In a medium bowl, combine all the ingredients and stir to blend.

Preheat the oven to 300 degrees F. In a large bowl, cream the butter and sugar together until light and fluffy, then gradually stir in the flour. Stir in the milk or water and orange-flower or rose water. On a lightly floured surface, knead until dough holds together and is easy to shape.

Pinch off a walnut-sized piece of dough. Roll it into a ball and hollow it out with your thumb. Pinch the sides up to form a pot shape. Place a spoonful of filling into the hollow, then pinch the dough closed over the filling. Press and score the sealed edge if desired. Bake until set but not browned, about 20 minutes. Carefully transfer to wire racks. While warm, dust heavily with confectioners' sugar.

Variation: Date-Filled Butter Cookies In a medium sauce-pan, combine 1 pound dates, pitted and chopped, with $^1/_2$ cup water. Bring to a simmer and cook to a paste, about 15 minutes. Stir in the grated zest of 1 orange and $^1/_2$ teaspoon ground cinnamon. Remove from heat and let cool. Use to stuff the dough, above.

: : : : : :

KNEGLETS, *or* KNADELS

MARZIPAN-FILLED COOKIES

These cookies go by many names, most of them affectionate. Algerian cook Emma Bensaid calls them *knedettes. Knadels,* or *kneglets,* appear in Fortunée Hazan-Arama's *Saveurs de mon enfance,* as well as in *La table juive* and Maguy Kakon's *La cuisine juive du Maroc de mère et fille.* Moroccan cooks sometimes call them *massapane* and use special molds that look like fluted tartlet molds. Small tartlet molds are a good idea, as forming the cookies by hand into stars is tricky and the dough has to set up properly to hold the star shape. Otherwise, the cookies spread out and lose their shape, although they taste delicious. Here's a case where practice makes perfect. These egg yolk and almond pastries are reminiscent of many Spanish and Portuguese sweets.

Makes 24 TO 30 *cookies*

For the dough:

4 CUPS SIFTED ALL-PURPOSE FLOUR

2 EGGS OR 4 EGG YOLKS, BEATEN

1/4 CUP CANOLA OIL

3 TABLESPOONS SUGAR

1/3 CUP FRESH ORANGE JUICE

1 OR 2 TABLESPOONS ORANGE-FLOWER WATER, OR TO TASTE

For the almond filling:

3 1/2 CUPS (1 1/4 POUNDS) BLANCHED ALMONDS

1 1/2 CUPS SUGAR

4 EGG YOLKS

GRATED ZEST OF 1 LEMON

VANILLA EXTRACT (OPTIONAL)

1 EGG WHITE AS NEEDED

CRYSTALLIZED OR COLORED SUGAR FOR SPRINKLING

To make the dough, in a large bowl, combine the flour, eggs or egg yolks, oil, sugar, orange juice, and the orange-flower water. Stir to make a firm dough. On a lightly floured work surface, roll the dough out to an 1/8-inch thickness.

With a glass or cookie cutter, cut into 2 1/2- to 3-inch rounds. Reroll the trimmings and cut out more rounds. Put the rounds on a clean towel and let rest for about 1 hour.

To make the filling, preheat the oven to 350 degrees F. In a food processor, grind the almonds. Add the sugar, egg yolks, lemon zest, and vanilla, if using, and mix well until you have a homogenous but not-too-stiff paste. If it is too firm, add the egg white.

Transfer the cookie rounds to parchment-lined baking sheets. On each cookie base, drop a generous spoonful or, if the mixture is firm enough to roll, a 1-inch round ball of almond paste. Pull the sides of the dough up and in, in small pleats, to form a 6-sided star. Sprinkle with crystallized or colored sugar. Bake until golden, 25 to 30 minutes. Let cool on wire racks. Store in an airtight container for up to 2 weeks.

Variation: Press balls of cookie dough to fit tiny tartlet molds. Fill the center with balls of almond paste. Bake as directed.

: : : : : :

GHORIBA *el* LOUZE

ALGERIAN ALMOND COOKIES

These sweet, chewy cookies are made from a classic marzipan that is baked and dipped in syrup. They can be made 1 week ahead of time and kept in a covered container.

Makes about 6 dozen cookies

3 CUPS (1 POUND) BLANCHED ALMONDS
$1^1/4$ CUPS SUGAR
1 TABLESPOON GRATED LEMON ZEST
2 EGGS, LIGHTLY BEATEN

For the syrup:
$^1/2$ CUP SUGAR
1 CUP WATER
1 TABLESPOON ORANGE-FLOWER WATER

2 CUPS CONFECTIONERS' SUGAR, SIFTED

Preheat the oven to 350 degrees F. In a blender or a food processor, grind the almonds and sugar together in batches. Pour into a medium bowl and stir in the zest. Make a well in the center and add the eggs. Mix well. Divide the mixture in half.

On a heavily floured work surface, roll each piece of dough into a rope about 18 inches long and $1^1/2$ inches in diameter. Flatten each rope into an oblong about 1 inch thick and cut on the diagonal into $1^1/2$-inch-thick slices. (Some versions roll the dough into walnut-sized balls, then flatten them slightly.)

Dust the slices with flour and place about 1 inch apart on parchment-lined or ungreased baking sheets. Bake until pale gold, about 15 minutes. Transfer to wire racks to cool.

To make the syrup, in a small saucepan, combine the sugar and water. Bring to a boil over high heat, stirring until the sugar dissolves. Cook, uncovered, until slightly thickened, about 10 minutes. Pour into a shallow bowl to cool. Add the orange-flower water. Spread the confectioners' sugar in a shallow pan. Dip each cookie in syrup, then sugar. Set on wire racks to dry.

: : : : : :

GORAYEBAH

PURIM BUTTER COOKIES

Very fragile and rich, these butter cookies are easy to assemble. While these are a Purim treat in Morocco, they are also quite nice with mint tea any day of the week.

Makes 30 TO 36 *cookies*

1½ CUPS (3 STICKS) UNSALTED BUTTER, AT ROOM
   TEMPERATURE
2 TABLESPOONS ORANGE-FLOWER WATER
1 CUP SUPERFINE SUGAR
3 CUPS SIFTED ALL-PURPOSE FLOUR
30 TO 36 BLANCHED WHOLE ALMONDS

Preheat the oven to 300 degrees F. In a large bowl, cream the butter until light and fluffy. Add the orange-flower water and sugar and beat well. Gradually stir in the flour. On a lightly floured work surface, knead the mixture until the dough holds together. Form into walnut-sized balls. Top each with an almond. Place 2 inches apart on parchment-lined or ungreased baking sheets. Bake until firm but not browned, 15 to 20 minutes. Transfer to wire racks to cool. Store in an airtight container for up to 1 week.

Variation: Lovers' Pastries In Syria, the dough is rolled into ropes and formed into a heart shape. Where the pieces join, they are topped with an almond. Some versions use confectioners' sugar rather than superfine.

: : : : : :

Le PAILLE

CEREMONIAL CAKE FROM MOROCCO

On special occasions such as weddings and bar mitzvahs, or holidays such as Purim, one spectacular cake is served, along with the small cookies, candies, and preserves. Its name—*le paille,* or more casually, *el pal* or *le pallebe*—comes from the English word *pie* and its base is *panaspana,* the classic sponge cake, or genoise. Usually assembled with four layers, it may be round or rectangular. A glaze and garnishes distinguish it from a simple frosted *panaspana.*

A similar cake is served in Algeria. In *The Architecture of Memory,* Joelle Bahloul quotes her cousin Clarisse talking about Purim: "'We would bake our cakes in a special oven. We'd spend the entire day at the oven. The day of the fast of Esther was the day for *biscuit de savoie* (sponge cake), and there was competition for who could bake the most beautiful cake. That was the custom. We'd eat this cake to break the fast . . . We'd beat up the eggs by hand. . . . they were such beautiful cakes.'"

The proportions and ingredients for the cake vary from recipe to recipe. For a dairy meal, you could use melted unsalted butter instead of oil. For Passover, the baking powder and flour would be eliminated and 1 cup ground almonds and ½ cup matzoh meal or potato starch would be used. Instead of the orange juice soaking mixture, some versions of the recipe use orange-flower water to melt the apricot jam, but I think that it is a bit overpowering. Chopped nuts are simmered in orange-flower water for another layer, and even the chocolate is melted with the orange-flower water. Wow! That's too intense for me.

You can make this as elegant or as baroque as you like. If ever there was a case for going over the top, this is it! (Remember that the plain cake is pretty good, too.)

Serves 12

For the genoise (panaspana) *cake:*

12 EGGS, SEPARATED

1³/4 CUPS SUGAR

¹/2 CUP CANOLA OIL, OR ¹/2 CUP (1 STICK) UNSALTED
   BUTTER, MELTED

¹/2 CUP FRESH ORANGE JUICE

GRATED ZEST OF 1 ORANGE (OPTIONAL)

2 TEASPOONS BAKING POWDER

2 CUPS ALL-PURPOSE FLOUR

For the glaze:

3 TABLESPOONS SUGAR

1 CUP FRESH ORANGE JUICE

¹/2 CUP RUM

For the filling:

2 CUPS ALMOND PASTE

²/3 CUP APRICOT OR BERRY JAM

2 CUPS CHOPPED FRESH FRUIT SUCH AS BERRIES,
   PEACHES, OR BANANAS

16 OUNCES SEMISWEET CHOCOLATE, CHOPPED

SILVER DRAGÉES AND SPRINKLES FOR DECORATION
   (OPTIONAL)

To make the cake, preheat the oven to 350 degrees F. Oil two 9-inch round or square cake pans (springform pans work well). Line the bottom with parchment paper and oil the parchment. Or, oil two 10-by-15-inch jelly-roll pans and line with parchment paper.

In a large bowl, beat the egg yolks and sugar until thick and pale. Beat in the oil or butter, orange juice, and zest, if using. In a large bowl, beat the egg whites until stiff, glossy peaks form. In a small bowl, combine the baking powder and flour. Stir to blend. Gradually whisk the flour mixture into the yolk mixture, then fold in the whites. Spoon the batter into the prepared pans.

Bake until the cake is golden, springy, and pulls away from the sides of the pans, 30 to 35 minutes; jelly-roll pans will take only 10 to 12 minutes. Let the cake cool, then turn out of the pans and peel off the parchment.

To assemble, cut each round or square horizontally into 2 layers. If you used jelly-roll pans, cut each cake crosswise to make 2 layers that measure 10 by 7¹/2 inches.

In a medium bowl, combine all the glaze ingredients.

To fill the cake, in a mixer, or by hand, knead the almond paste until it is softened. Set aside. In a small saucepan, heat the jam over low heat until melted. Place the first cake layer on a serving platter. Drizzle it with one-fourth of the glaze. Spread this layer thinly with the warm melted jam. Place another layer of cake on top of the bottom layer. Drizzle with the same amount of glaze. Then top this layer with the chopped fruit. Top this with the third layer of cake, then drizzle with the same amount of glaze. Spread the top with the almond paste. Place the last layer on top and pour over the remaining glaze.

In a double boiler, melt the chocolate over barely simmering water. While warm, pour over the cake. Decorate with dragées and sprinkles, if you like.

Variation: For a simple presentation, frost the cake with a mixture of 1¹/2 cups sifted confectioners' sugar beaten with 5 egg whites and flavored with a bit of lemon juice.

: : : : : :

SFENJ

MOROCCAN HANUKKAH DONUTS

On Hanukkah, the Festival of Lights, fried foods are served to celebrate the oil lamp that burned for eight miraculous nights. These Moroccan donuts are usually dipped in warm honey, but you can use granulated sugar as well. (Similar fritters, called *yoyo* in Tunisia, are made with an egg dough that is leavened with baking powder instead of yeast and is perfumed with vanilla and orange zest.) The dough is easier to work with if you add the eggs and a bit of oil or melted margarine. These *sfenj* are scented with orange zest as well as orange juice. In Israel, Hanukkah donuts are filled with jelly and called *sufganiyot*.

Makes about 20 donuts

2 ENVELOPES ACTIVE DRY YEAST

$1/4$ CUP SUGAR

$1/2$ CUP WARM WATER

4 CUPS ALL-PURPOSE FLOUR

$1/2$ TEASPOON SALT

2 EGGS, LIGHTLY BEATEN (OPTIONAL)

GRATED ZEST OF 1 ORANGE

$1/4$ CUP CANOLA OIL, MELTED MARGARINE, OR MELTED
    UNSALTED BUTTER (OPTIONAL)

$1^1/2$ TO 2 CUPS WARM WATER OR PART WATER, PART
    ORANGE JUICE

PEANUT OR CANOLA OIL FOR DEEP-FRYING

GRANULATED SUGAR FOR SPRINKLING OR WARM HONEY
    FOR DIPPING

Dissolve the yeast and sugar in the water. Let sit until foamy, about 10 minutes. Pour into a large bowl and gradually stir in the flour and salt. Stir in the eggs, zest, and $1/4$ cup oil, margarine, or butter, if using. Stir in just enough water or water and juice

to make a soft and elastic dough. Knead well, with a dough hook or by hand on a lightly floured surface, until the dough is elastic, smooth, and shiny. Roll the dough into a ball, place in an oiled bowl, and turn to coat. Cover with a damp towel or plastic wrap and let rise in a warm place until doubled, $1^1/2$ to 2 hours.

Oil your hands. Divide the dough into 20 balls about 2 inches in diameter. In a deep saucepan or wok, heat 3 inches of oil to 365 degrees F. Take a ball of dough, make a hole in the center, and pull it out to make a donut shape. Deep-fry a few at a time until the donuts are puffed and golden. Using a slotted spoon or skimmer, transfer to paper towels to drain. While still hot, sprinkle with granulated sugar or dip in warm honey. Serve warm.

: : : : : :

CIGARES *aux* AMANDES, *or* BRIKS *aux* AMANDES

ALMOND CIGARS

Moroccans and Tunisians are fond of these flaky nut-filled sweets. In Algeria, they are served after the Yom Kippur fast, but the filling omits ginger, cloves, and orange-flower water and uses simply almonds, sugar, lemon, and cinnamon. Some are filled with walnuts instead of almonds. These may also be called *briouats*.

Makes 24 pastries

For the filling:

4 CUPS (1^1/$_3$ POUNDS) BLANCHED ALMONDS, TOASTED
    AND COARSELY CHOPPED
1^1/$_2$ CUPS SUGAR
1 TEASPOON GROUND GINGER
1 TEASPOON GROUND CLOVES
1 TEASPOON GROUND CINNAMON
2 EGG YOLKS
1 TABLESPOON ORANGE-FLOWER WATER
1 EGG WHITE AS NEEDED

12 *FEUILLES DE BRIK,* OR 24 SQUARE EGG ROLL
    WRAPPERS, OR 1 POUND FILO DOUGH
1 EGG WHITE, LIGHTLY BEATEN, IF USING *FEUILLES DE*
    BRIK OR EGG ROLL WRAPPERS
^{3}/$_4$ CUP (1^1/$_2$ STICKS) BUTTER OR MARGARINE, MELTED
    IF USING FILO
PEANUT OIL FOR DEEP-FRYING
^{3}/$_4$ CUP ORANGE BLOSSOM HONEY

To make the filling, in a food processor, grind the almonds and sugar together in batches. Pulse in the spices, egg yolks, and orange-flower water. If

the paste is too dry, add the egg white. Divide into 24 balls of almond paste. (Tunisians add a bit of semolina to the filling.)

If using *feuilles de brik* or egg roll wrappers: Cut the *feuilles de brik* in half. Place a strip of filling along one side, tuck in the edges, roll into a cigar shape, and seal the edges with egg white.

If using filo: Cut the filo into 6-by-12-inch rectangles. Stack in 3 layers, brushing each layer with butter or margarine. Add the filling, tuck in the ends of the filo, and roll up like a cigar.

In a Dutch oven or deep fryer, heat 3 inches of oil to 375 degrees F. In a small saucepan, warm the honey. Fry the cigars in batches. Using a skimmer, transfer to paper towels to drain, then dip in warm honey.

Variation: Leone Jaffin's Substitute this filling for the one above: In a large saucepan, melt 2 cups sugar over medium heat. Stir in 3 cups ground almonds, ^{1}/$_2$ teaspoon ground cinnamon, and the grated zest of 2 lemons. In place of warmed honey, use this syrup: In a medium saucepan, combine ^{1}/$_4$ cup honey, ^{1}/$_4$ cup sugar, the grated zest and juice of 1 lemon, and ^{1}/$_2$ cup water. Bring to a boil and simmer for 5 minutes. Use warm.

Note: Filo *cigares* may also be baked in a preheated 350 degree F oven for 30 minutes.

BIBLIOGRAPHY

Abdennour, Samia. *Egyptian Cooking: A Practical Guide*. New York: Hippocrene Books, 1998.

Angel, Gilda. *Sephardic Holiday Cooking*. Mt. Vernon and New York: Decalogue Books, 1986.

Bahloul, Joelle. *The Architecture of Memory: A Jewish-Muslim Household in Colonial Algeria 1937–1962*. Cambridge: Press Syndicate, University of Cambridge, 1992.

———. *La culte de la table dressée: rites et traditions de la table juive algérienne*. Paris: A. M. Metailie, 1983.

Blady, Ken. *Jewish Communities in Exotic Places*. Northvale, New Jersey: Jason Aronson, 2000.

Chiche-Yana, Martine. *La table juive: recettes et traditions du cycle de vie*. Aix-en-Provence: Edisud, 1994.

———. *La table juive: recettes et traditions de Fêtes*. Aix-en-Provence: Edisud, 1992.

Cohen-Azuelos, Jacqueline. *Fleur de safran: images et saveurs du Maroc*. Aix-en-Provence: Edisud, 1999.

Cooper, John. *Eat and Be Satisfied*. Northvale, New Jersey and London: Jason Aronson, 1993.

Corey, Helen. *The Art of Syrian Cookery*. Garden City and New York: Doubleday and Company, 1962.

Danan, Simy, and Jacques Denardaud. *La nouvelle cuisine judeo-marocaine*. Paris: ACR Edition, 1994.

der Haroutunian, Arto. *North African Cookery*. London: Century Publishing, 1985.

Farah, Madelain. *Lebanese Cuisine*. P.O. Box 66395, Portland, Oregon, 1991.

Ganz Perez, Helene. *Marrakech la rouge: les juifs de la medina*. Geneva: Editions Metropolis, 1996.

Guinaudeau, Zette. *Traditional Moroccan Cooking*. London: Serif, 1994.

Hazan-Arama, Fortunée. *Saveurs de mon enfance: la cuisine juive du Maroc*. Paris: Editions Robert Laffont, 1987.

Helou, Anissa. *Lebanese Cuisine*. London: Grub Street, 1994.

Ifergan, Jeanne. *Savoir préparer la cuisine juive d'Afrique du Nord*. Paris: Crealivers, 1990.

Jaffin, Leone. *150 recettes et mille et un souvenirs d'une juive d'Algérie*. Paris: Editions Encre, 1996.

Kaak, Zeinab. *La sofra: cuisine tunisienne traditionelle*. Tunis: Ceres Editions, 1995.

Kakon, Maguy. *La cuisine juive du Maroc de mère et fille*. Panayrac: Editions Daniel Briand, n.d.

Kouki, Mohamed. *Cuisine et patisserie tunisienne*. Tunis: La Société d'Arts Graphiques d'Edition et de Presse, 1987.

Laasri, Ahmed. *240 recettes de cuisine marocaine*. Paris: Jacques Grancher, 1982.

Morse, Kitty. *Come with Me to the Kasbah: A Cook's Tour of Morocco*. Casablanca: Editions Serar, 1989.

Moryoussef, Viviane and Nina Moryoussef. *Moroccan Jewish Cookery*. Paris and Casablanca: J. P. Taillandier, Sochepresse, 1983.

Nadja. *Arabic Cook Book*. Berkeley, California: Women of the Middle East, 1961.

Rayess, George N. *Rayess' Art of Lebanese Cooking*. Beirut: Librairie du Liban, 1966.

Roden, Claudia. *The Book of Jewish Food*. New York: Alfred A. Knopf, 1996.

Rodrigue, Aron. *Images of Sefardi and Eastern Jeweries in Transition: The Teachers of the Alliance Israelite Universelle, 1860–1939*. Seattle and London: University of Washington Press, 1993.

Salloum, Hajeeb, and Peters, James. *From the Lands of Figs and Olives*. New York: Interlink Books, 1995.

Scheindlin, Raymond P. *A Short History of the Jewish People: From Legendary Times to Modern Statehood*. New York: Macmillan, 1998.

Taieb, Daisy. *Les fêtes juives à Tunis racontées à mes filles*. Nice: Epsilon, 1998.

Taieb, Jacques. *Être juif au Maghreb à la vielle de la colonisation*. Paris: Editions Albin Michel, 1994.

Tamzali, Haydee. *La cuisine en Afrique du Nord*. Paris: Vilo Press, 1986.

Vallero, Rina. *Delights of Jerusalem*. Tel Aviv: Nahar Publishing House, 1985.

Wolfert, Paula. *Mediterranean Greens and Grains*. New York: HarperCollins, 1998.

———. *Mediterranean Cooking*. Rev. ed. New York: Harper Perennial, 1994.

Wright, Clifford. *A Mediterranean Feast*. New York: William Morrow, 1999.

Zana-Murat, Andrée. *De mère et fille la cuisine juive tunisienne*. Paris: Albin Michel, 1998.

Zeitoun, Edmond. *250 recettes de cuisine tunisienne*. Paris: Jacques Grancher, 1977.

INDEX

TABLE OF EQUIVALENTS

LIQUID AND DRY MEASURES

U.S.	METRIC
1/4 teaspoon	1.25 milliliters
1/2 teaspoon	2.5 milliliters
1 teaspoon	5 milliliters
1 tablespoon (3 teaspoons)	15 milliliters
1 fluid ounce (2 tablespoons)	30 milliliters
1/4 cup	60 milliliters
1/3 cup	80 milliliters
1 cup	120 milliliters
1 pint (2 cups)	480 milliliters
1 quart (4 cups, 32 ounces)	960 milliliters
1 gallon (4 quarts)	3.84 liters
1 ounce (by weight)	28 grams
1 pound	454 grams
2.2 pounds	1 kilogram

OVEN TEMPERATURES

FAHRENHEIT	CELSIUS	GAS
250	120	1/2
275	140	1
300	150	2
325	160	3
350	180	4
375	190	5
400	200	6
425	220	7
450	230	8
475	240	9
500	260	10

LENGTH MEASURES

U.S.	METRIC
1/8 inch	3 millimeters
1/4 inch	6 millimeters
1/2 inch	12 millimeters
1 inch	2.5 centimeters

The exact equivalents in the above tables have been rounded for convenience.

ACKNOWLEDGMENTS

As usual many thanks to my wonderful editor Bill LeBlond for his support, intelligence, and finesse. Also at Chronicle Books, thank you Amy Treadwell and Jan Hughes for eagle vision and attention to detail, and to Michele Fuller and Sarah Bailey for marketing savvy. Thank you to copy editor Carolyn Miller.

This book is beautiful thanks to the talents of designer Sara Schneider, photographer Leigh Beisch, stylist Sandra Cook, and prop stylist Sara Slavin. Bravo!

Thanks to Gary Woo and Barbara Haimes for cooking some of this food with me at special event dinners. Your finely tuned palates and perfectionism helped refine the recipes.

Thanks for Greg Drescher at the CIA for inviting me to participate in those wonderfully educational Mediterranean conferences.

Thanks to Oldways Preservation and Exchange Trust for the amazing trip to Morocco.

Thanks to Chef Abderrazak Haouari for the opportunity for cooking collaboration and for sharing his recipes and palate.

Again, thanks to family and friends for being expert tasters and critics.

Special thanks to Mark Furstenberg and Anne Tyler for culinary savvy and friendship.